WORDS UNSPOKEN

Words Unspoken

An Invitation to Christian Faith

PETER SCHMIECHEN

CASCADE *Books* • Eugene, Oregon

WORDS UNSPOKEN
An Invitation to Christian Faith

Copyright © 2012 Peter Schmiechen. All rights reserved. Except for brief quotations in critical publications or reviews, no part of this book may be reproduced in any manner without prior written permission from the publisher. Write: Permissions, Wipf and Stock Publishers, 199 W. 8th Ave., Suite 3, Eugene, OR 97401.

Cascade Books
An Imprint of Wipf and Stock Publishers
199 W. 8th Ave., Suite 3
Eugene, OR 97401

www.wipfandstock.com

ISBN 13: 978-1-62032-184-3

Cataloging-in-Publication data:

Schmiechen, Peter.

    Words unspoken : an invitation to Christian faith / Peter Schmiechen.

    xii + 116 p. ; 23 cm.

    ISBN 13: 978-1-62032-184-3

    1. Christianity—Essence, genius, nature. 2. Theology, Doctrinal—Popular works. I. Title.

BT77 .S365 2012

Manufactured in the U.S.A.

In Gratitude to
Samuel and Marie Schmiechen; Carl and Bernice Hoffman

In Love for
Jan
Tim and Betsy, Will and Erin
Nate and Malinda, Alex and Zoe

"For I handed on to you as of first importance
what I in turn had received. . ."
1 CORINTHIANS 15:3

Table of Contents

Welcome ix

PART ONE *Origins*

1. Speaking of Christian Faith 3
2. The Story of Jesus 6
3. The Messenger 10
4. Resistance 12
5. Grace 16
6. Justice 21
7. Compassion 26
8. Faith 31
9. Light 40
10. Purpose 47

PART TWO *Reflections*

11. Naming Jesus 55
12. Sin 66
13. Good News 74
14. The Church as the Community of Christ 83
15. Sacraments: The Bonds of Love 92
16. The Living God 100
17. Conclusion 108

Welcome

BY THE GRACE OF God, my wife and I raised two sons. We love them dearly and are extremely proud of them. And, as I approach the three quarters of a century mark, I find myself drawn repeatedly to words unspoken. Somehow I have not taken the opportunity to communicate directly to them the substance of the faith, hope, and love embedded in Christian communities. The problem is not the absence of love in their lives, a lack of moral discipline, or a lack of passion for the common good. It is rather that the connections between these values and the community of Christ were not made explicit.

How could this happen? Our sons were born in the 1960s. While they did not fully experience those turbulent times, they grew up in a culture overwhelmed by the change and conflict of that period. All traditional institutions and values came under attack and suffered greatly—too often for good reason. It was not a time to embrace traditions with an uncritical eye. For all sorts of reasons, the moral values we prized were uncoupled from the church. But as much as one might turn this subject into a diatribe against all that is wrong with church and culture, that would only turn attention away from the positive purpose envisioned here, namely, that at this point in my life and my relation with my sons, there are things still unspoken.

To say this is to admit that my wife and I made mistakes as parents. We were educated in the optimism of the fifties and early sixties. In the endless debate regarding freedom and order, we wanted faith and moral values to be claimed freely. After all, the creed rightly begins with the words "I believe . . ." not "My parents forced me . . ." So while we sought to nurture habits of the heart in family and churchly practices, we also gave our children freedom to grow in their own ways. We also assumed that the network of people and institutions in our lives (extended family, schools,

Welcome

church, college, arts, literature, and social commentary) would support our personal goals for our sons. In retrospect we now can see that each of these parts of our inhabited world varied greatly in their willingness and ability to nurture religious experience and/or values. For example, by the 1980s the liberal arts colleges they attended saw less and less reason to engender the knowledge of the religious traditions that shaped our culture. The formation of faith was no longer considered a vital part of liberal education. To be sure, arts, music, and literature cultivate religious sensitivities. But one must make decisions to look, listen, and read in specific places and be provided some guidance. A tour of a great gallery or cathedral, going to a Handel or Brahms choral concert and reading great expressions of the human spirit—all are practices which must be carefully nurtured. We succeeded in cultivating these interests but without much support from the larger culture.

Generally speaking, one could argue that in spite of all the upheavals in our culture our sons have claimed the family values. Given the fact that religion in America has been used to justify all manner of injustice and defend the idols of this world, their caution in things religious may mean that they learned their lessons quite well from both parents. It will also be helpful to see their relation to organized religion as symptomatic of their culture. They are not the only forty-something adults from several generations not participating in religion. It may well be that the anxiety of their father is caused by his preoccupation with things theological and that they know more and believe more than they reveal. Whether the problem lies in the sorry state of religion in America during the past fifty years, or in the need for the grandfather of their children to speak before it is too late, in either case it is time to offer these words on religion yet unspoken.

It is against this background that I invite you into a conversation regarding Christian faith. While the origin of these chapters lies in our family and there are a few family references, it is not a private family conversation. It is written for those disconnected from the church. Some of you were raised in churches but left as teenagers. Some were pushed out and became refugees because of outrageous actions by churches. (Yes, churches are too often their worst enemy!) Still others have never known much about Christian faith, except for what can be gathered from the general culture—which is not always the best recommendation. This is obviously a wide range of readers. I have tried to write in plain English,

Welcome

without lapsing into technical jargon. At the same time I refuse to dumb down the discussion or appeal to crass interests. I have assumed that you are bright and care about people and our society, that issues of identity, human relations, moral values, and the common good concern you. I also assume that the story of Jesus has its own power to attract and point to a new future for all of us. So I shall ask you to consider crucial points in that story. If at times I get involved in telling these stories, it is because the story is the important thing. As the title says, this is an invitation to Christian faith.

I have been encouraged to pursue this project by family and friends—including my two sons—and am most grateful. These conversations persuaded me that our family experience reflects a larger cultural situation affecting many families. I also wish to thank the staff at Wipf and Stock Publishers for their interest and support as the manuscript made its way through the process: Christian Amondson, Assistant Managing Editor; Heather Carraher, Lead Production Editor; and Rodney Clapp, Editor.

PART ONE

Origins

1

Speaking of Christian Faith

I WANT TO SPEAK of Christian faith. To be sure, we could easily begin by speaking of religion, since the Christian faith is a religion. Many have done so in helpful ways. Here, however, I want to begin with a general image of Christian faith. In another context I would be prepared to engage in historical analysis to show that this image is consistent with what is at the heart of Christianity. But not now. As they say in politics, I want to stay on message and speak of a vision of Christian faith we might share.

Being Christian is risky business. It involves a broken heart and great joy. It calls us to live a kind of double life: to see and experience the brokenness of life, which means to bear great sorrow and practice compassion; but also to see and experience new life born of grace, which means to know great joy and practice hope. We are not talking about neutral facts unrelated to our lives, but the most heartfelt contradiction in our own lives and the state of the world. We see a world of earthquakes and floods, disease and death, acts of unspeakable ill will and violence, and of course the aches and pains reminding us of our own finitude. We also see wonderful gifts of life in new birth and daily food, friendship and love, acts of human creativity and the beauty of nature. We suffer and we rejoice. To be Christian is to claim both and live in the midst of opposites, tensions, and contradictions. The tensions are not simply out there but in us. We ourselves experience the limitations of our bodies, our moral strivings, and our efforts to be at peace with ourselves and one another. But what is decisive is that Christian faith is born in the conviction that we are claimed by a saving power which allows us to see the world with joy and hope.

There is, of course, another solution to this problem if we are willing to affirm only one side of the contradiction. We could, for example, admit that life really is filled with terrifying events and ends up at the graveyard. The sorrow is so real that there is not much else to say. Or, with a little bit of denial and a lot of optimism, we might declare that only the good is real. On these terms, we may need some help in positive thinking, but if we work at it by isolating ourselves in a community of good things, we may even convince ourselves that life has only *happy endings*. Christian faith rejects both of these solutions and, as a consequence, complicates things all the more. Why it insists on affirming both sides of the contradiction, and how it is resolved, goes to the heart of Christian faith. For now, the point is that Christian existence is knowing that in the midst of great sorrow, we are claimed by a grace which offers gifts of love and hope. The limits and contradictions are not eliminated but we no longer believe that they are the last word.

Perhaps this approach helps us understand why Christian faith can be described in diametrically opposing ways. It is not uncommon to hear that the world is a paradise lost, a fallen existence, caught in the powers of sin, death, and Satan. Some choose to speak of human existence as alienated from its true form, or divided between conflicting goals, or even suffering an incurable sickness. Such pessimistic comments are matched by positive affirmations of new life, freedom from all that would control us, restoration as daughters and sons of God, children of light, and heirs to the promises of God. It is not surprising that critics have latched on to the description of sorrows to paint a negative picture of Christian faith, or that some Christians are so tired of hearing about the sorrows that they want to speak only of positive things.

I admit that my view of Christian life is a tragic one. By this I do not mean that we are predetermined to fail and endure sorrow, but that in spite of the goodness of creation and our good intentions, we find ourselves in the midst of great sorrows. To avoid this observation astounds me. I can not explain how it can happen without wondering if there is a lack of moral sensitivity, a practice of denial, or outright dishonesty. To suggest these things sounds very harsh. But what else can you call the attempt to avoid a realistic look at the world as it is? The attempt requires the creation of a fantasy land removed from the real world. To be sure, the tragic view always lives in the shadow of despair and this may be why some do not want to visit Disneyland but live there. In contrast, Christianity is hopeful not by denying sorrow, but by passing through it to new life born of grace. All of this is to say that Christians live between Good Friday and Easter. If the former portrays all of the sorrow of this world, the latter affirms God's vindication of all who suffer for righteousness sake. But the key is that there is no way to get to Easter without going through Good Friday. As the saying goes: no cross, no crown.

2

The Story of Jesus

WHERE DO WE START? During the last two centuries Christians have spent a great deal of time thinking about this question. The answers are many and varied. Does one start at the beginning and talk about God the Creator? Or, if that is not back far enough, does one first have to establish the existence of God before we can talk about anything? Do we start with some claim to an impartial reason, appeal to the authority of the Bible or church doctrine, or as some prefer, with our own experience? I have spent my life working with these options and am not going to review them.

To give some indication of where I am on the great theological map, let me say that I don't think we can prove the existence of God. Since the Bible and doctrine are witnesses to what God is doing in our lives, I would prefer to begin there. On the first page of his great work, John Calvin (sixteenth-century Protestant Reformer) declared that theological knowledge consists of the knowledge of God and the knowledge of ourselves. He then added the most insightful comment that it is not always clear which comes first. He did not mean that we are more important than God, but rather that our thoughts move back and forth between serious reflection about our lives and God. Each informs the other, each raises objections, each gives a measure of new insight. Hidden in this comment is also a warning: there is no one correct way to begin talking about Christian faith. As you can attest, you have lived with a father who can see something while driving and launch into a comment about God! Things in this world point to God in unusual ways and God allows us to

The Story of Jesus

see them in new ways. Likewise, to know God is to discover a reality that is largely unimaginable from a human perspective, so that our thoughts about God are always being revised.

I want to begin this conversation of God and ourselves by using the story of Jesus. As noted above, there is no getting around or beyond Jesus. But I owe you a brief heads-up on the special meanings attached to the phrase *the story of Jesus*, which is very popular in theological writings today. At one level, this affirms that when we speak about the meaning of Christian faith, it is best to speak about Jesus—what he does and who he is. This is in contrast to attempts to prove the existence of God, offer logical deductions from abstract ideas, or jump into church doctrines. This has always been one way Christians have explained the faith, as the New Testament makes clear. It was revived by the Reformers in the sixteenth century and continues in various forms to this day as the dominant way Protestants do theology. Since it makes no claim to have discovered some universal starting point that will persuade all people, but speaks from the standpoint of the community of faith, it is often called a *confessional* approach. It admits that it can only confess what we believe.

At a second level, the phrase ("the story of Jesus") signals that we are going to talk about Jesus in a particular way, namely by means of story or narrative, rather than logical analysis of great ideas, ethical teachings, or the technical language of doctrines. Consider the way the word *narrative* is used today in political life. Commentators note how a leader gains an advantage by offering a compelling narrative of what is happening. We identify with narratives because they are personal and include us. They draw us into the world of the speaker and help us understand what is happening. This, we are told, works better than a speech with eight basic principles, defined and argued. As one candidate in 2011 discovered, it is also very easy to forget what the third point is! So a powerful narrative is deemed much better. Well, so with theological discourse. (It took us a while to discover that the Bible is mostly narrative, but we finally got the message.) So, by asking you to hear the *story* of Jesus, you are being asked to hear an open-ended narrative that hopefully will invite you into his world but also become the story of your life.

This brings us to yet another level: telling and hearing stories is complex. We do not have the resources to write a biography of Jesus from birth to death. Instead we have four Gospels, or proclamations of good news, about Jesus. These reflect what the first communities remembered

Part One: Origins

about Jesus and—most important—what they considered to be decisive in depicting what God had done to and for them in Jesus. This means that these portrayals of Jesus are very selective and clearly represent themes the authors, and their communities, wanted to emphasize. Thus there are differences between the four Gospels, with gaps in the story. For several centuries the critical study of the Gospels has worked on these problems producing many negative conclusions (for example, suggesting that the birth narratives are what we would call symbolic or legendary, or that the writers inserted sayings into the mouth of Jesus). This so alarmed people that they began to wonder if we can speak of Jesus at all. Others responded by going into complete denial, rejecting all critical discussion in order to preserve a literal reading of the Gospels. As a poster advertising a Christmas pageant declared: "Come to the Christmas play and see how it actually happened." There will always be naïve literalism and the critical debates will go on forever. But what is interesting in our time is the emergence of a handful of scholars who accept many of the limitations of the Gospels but have produced amazingly positive conclusions about what we can say about Jesus. They have affirmed good news not by denying the problems but working in the face of them. (I think there is a lesson there.)

To begin with the story of Jesus, then, is to see how Jesus was remembered. This concedes that the story tells us something about the early Christians as well as something about Jesus. When the story portrays Jesus as teacher, wonder worker, prophet, witness to God's Kingdom, and the anointed of God who was faithful unto death, we need to ask: what does this say about Jesus and what does it say about those who chose to remember him this way? And lest I forget, there is another line of remembrance contained in the story which I will often bring up, namely, how they remember themselves. If all this is not enough, there is yet another aspect to telling the story of Jesus: why do *we* tell it and *how and why do we respond* to it? In other words, we are inevitably brought into the story and will have to deal with how our stories relate to the story of Jesus.

Religious art illustrates the point. Medieval paintings of scenes from the Gospels are usually set in medieval times. The artist chooses to remember a particular scene and in the process paints his world into it. The viewers, therefore, are looking at Jesus and the disciples, but also themselves. Or consider how Jesus has been depicted in art in terms of the human features of the ancient Middle East, all parts of Europe from the Mediterranean to Scandinavia, as well as Africa and the Far East. The story is about Jesus but it inevitably becomes a story about ourselves: what we remember, what we tell, where we see ourselves in it and how we react. So, let me tell you a story about Jesus.

3

The Messenger

St. Mark begins his Gospel by announcing that it is about the good news of Jesus Christ, the Son of God. He then quotes from the Old Testament prophet Isaiah about God sending a messenger to prepare the way of the Lord. This introduces John the Baptist, an itinerant preacher who called people to repentance and the forgiveness of sins by baptism. Then Jesus appears. When he is baptized by John, the Spirit descends on Jesus and a voice from heaven declares: "Thou art my beloved Son, with thee I am well pleased." The Spirit then drives Jesus into the wilderness where he remains for forty days and is tempted by Satan. When he returns to Galilee he announces: "The Kingdom of God is at hand; repent, and believe in the gospel."

All of that happens in fifteen verses, in a compact style typical of Mark. Unlike Matthew and Luke, Mark does not begin with birth narratives. So what is going on? To begin with, don't be sidetracked by the titles "Son of God" or "beloved Son." In this context they do not mean a divine being, but more likely, a chosen or anointed one, even a messenger. Given the fact that this introduction has John deferring to Jesus, followed by baptism, temptations, and ends with Jesus' proclamation of the Kingdom of God, I think it is appropriate to think of Jesus as the messenger. It helps us focus on the real issue. Why is Jesus anointed with the Spirit? In order to proclaim the Kingdom of God. But to be God's messenger he must first be empowered by the Spirit and overcome temptations. Remember that *Messiah* in Hebrew and *Christos* in Greek mean anointed. Jesus is anointed as God's messenger.

Messenger is a powerful title because it points in several directions: what is the message, who is sending it, and to whom is it directed. By declaring that the message is about the Kingdom of God, Jesus points us in the direction of Jewish faith in a God who creates and redeems Israel. This takes us back to Moses and the covenant of trust and love between God and Israel. It invokes the prophetic words of judgment against all the things that break the covenant: mistrust, misuse of people and things, and forsaking God in favor of the comforts and idols of this world. Like John's message, it begins with a call to repentance but is filled with hope: the God of the covenant is merciful and God's loving kindness endures forever. So, by invoking the image of the Kingdom or Rule of God on earth, Jesus is at once calling people back to the tradition of trust in God alone. But he is also raising expectations that such a God can and will redeem the people even in this time of Roman rule and endless conspiracies between local leaders and powers in Rome. What it all means and how it will happen are things Mark will fill in later, but for now, the message is about the Rule of God.

This answer opens a new perspective on the story of Jesus. When we started I said I wanted to tell the story of Jesus. So why are we now talking about God? Is this some kind of theological trick? Well, actually the story is supposed to be about Jesus and in fact it is. But Jesus is important to the Gospel writers and Christians in general because he is the messenger of God. So in this sense I have to admit that the real subject of the Gospels is God: the one who sends Jesus, who becomes evident to people in the face of Jesus, in his words, in his welcome, and in his own personal trust of God. Of course this creates something of a disparity: in, through, and with the struggles of people worn out by hard times and the Romans, we catch glimpses of a divine purpose. For the Jewish perspective, this is the way it has always been in the stories of Abraham, Moses leading the Jews out of bondage in Egypt, Nathan the prophet confronting David, or other prophets denouncing those who have no regard for widows and orphans. In this case, God turns up in the words of John and Jesus as they declare that in this strange place and time God shall appear to do a new thing.

But to whom is the message directed? That is a question to be answered in many ways in what follows.

4

Resistance

THE MESSAGE IS DIRECTED to anyone who will listen. That creates problems, because sometimes the wrong people pay attention; at other times some don't like what Jesus says or how he says it. If one does not like the message one can always find ways to object to the process. So Jesus is in trouble for associating with the wrong people, for false teaching, and for claiming authority. Let's gather all these reactions to Jesus and put them into a box marked Resistance. In the Gospels resistance takes many forms.

The simplest form occurs among the disciples, as they appear to be incapable of understanding what Jesus is saying. They don't understand his teachings and assume he is talking the language of power politics: with Jesus they will turn the tables on those who now have wealth and power. Peter refuses to accept that Jesus as the messenger must suffer. Jesus uses their resistance as the occasion to propose just the opposite. When the disciples want to relegate women and children to the background, Jesus welcomes them. When the disciples voice prejudice against Samaritans, Jesus elevates Samaritans to equal status. In later sections I will use other examples of the disciples' resistance to highlight what Jesus is saying.

Mark introduces a benign form of resistance in order to create dramatic tension. After Jesus announces the coming of the Kingdom, he moves around engaging people with his teaching, reading from the Book of Isaiah in a local synagogue, and healing several people. All of these events cause people to ask who Jesus is, but they don't know. Instead of offering titles, each story ends with the simple note that people were astonished. This fits into Mark's way of telling the story. He wants us to stand with the spectators, hear what happened, and wonder who Jesus is. But then he finally has someone declare who Jesus is, but it is not a disciple or follower, or someone in authority. It is a poor man possessed by demons, forced to live alone in the cemetery. This man, the very one held in bondage by demonic power, knows who Jesus is. Ordinary folk can't figure it out, but those aligned with the devil see Jesus coming and resist his power.

[Time Out: In the modern world the healings have been called miracles, which only creates problems. In the scientific outlook of the modern age, *miracle* has come to mean a violation of the natural order, which operates according to fixed rules that we can understand. So if one encounters something one cannot explain, some would call it a miracle. As you can imagine, this leads to the confrontation between the claim of miracles and modern science, which is impossible to resolve. But perhaps more important, if the unusual acts cannot be explained or understood, we can hardly infer that God did them. In fact, in one story the crowd suggests that it is the devil doing these things through Jesus. By contrast it would be more helpful to see in the healings a sign or wonder which could be interpreted in different ways. This is more consistent with the way the Old Testament presents acts of God. They are seldom self-evident but require interpretation.]

The Gospel of John shows us a different kind of resistance: instead of disagreeing with what Jesus says, sometimes people simply do not comprehend. For example, a teacher cannot comprehend that the change God works in us is like a second birth. He assumes Jesus is speaking literally and asks about the mechanics of a person being born again. This is followed by two somewhat amusing examples of not comprehending: when Jesus offers the Samaritan woman *living water*, she questions how he can do that since he has no jar to hold water; when Jesus offers the disciples the *bread of life* they ask one another whether he has been to market to buy bread. I think these examples of not understanding speak to our situation. In John, the cases involve looking at the world as if it were flat, i.e., what you see is what you get, the world is all there is, there is no depth, mystery or special meaning in anything. Such a mindset resists religious language because such language speaks of God in and through things of this world. Things can point beyond themselves to their Creator; words can possess spiritual power to awaken in us new life. As long as we think

Part One: Origins

the world is flat, we don't even get to the moral question: do I want to be re-born, do I want living water or the bread of life? We can't get to that level because we do not comprehend the images. For so much of our culture, where worldly stuff is everything, John's Gospel is a wake-up call. John ridicules a kind of spiritual blindness, a total lack of imagination, that leaves us stranded in a flat world.

Let me add a comment to this discussion of people caught in a flat world. You are probably wanting to ask: If so many people live in a flat world, why is science fiction and fantasy so popular? One answer is that for many in a flat world, such forms are not popular. *Lord of the Rings* and the Harry Potter stories are nonsense. If they are true flat-landers, and have no interest in any kind of imaginative stories, they really are confined to flat language. But what about the people who love such fiction? It would appear that these forms give expression to the imagination at a time when we are asked to take worldly things so seriously. The moral and religious implications of much of this fiction are so great that one wonders if these books meet all sorts of other needs. After all, Harry Potter is a story—did you get that, a narrative—about a boy, saved by the sacrifice of a loving mother, who must now devote his life to overcome evil. Well, it would appear that our world is not entirely filled with flat thinking. But yes, there are some who think the Harry Potter stories are bad because they depict witchcraft.

Returning to the resistance in the Gospels, we need to consider the resistance present in temptations and conflict with demonic powers. Three writers make clear that Jesus cannot be the messenger unless he overcomes temptations. And the Gospels go out of their way to admit that the struggle with temptation continues to the very end. When Jesus prays in the Garden of Gethsemene before his arrest, he voices the desire to avoid the impending conflict before finally committing himself to the will of God. No doubt the portrayal of such temptations of Jesus was extremely important for the early Christians as they encountered resistance of all kinds, including persecution.

From many different sources, Jesus meets resistance to his message. In some cases it is found in criticism of what he says or does. When he heals a man it is suggested that he has such power because he himself is connected to demonic powers. At other times he takes flack because he heals on the Sabbath. Some like to ask him trick questions about sick people and sin, or divorce, or paying taxes to Caesar. The questions are launched in the expectation that Jesus will give the wrong answer and arouse opposition. That Jesus is able to maneuver through these mine fields without disaster only makes some more upset, leading to the final confrontation in the last week when he arrives in Jerusalem. At this point the resistance takes the form of opposition, arrest, and death by execution.

Given the terrible events at the close of Jesus' life, it should not surprise us that at least two Gospel writers (Matthew and Luke) choose to incorporate frightening warnings at the beginnings of their Gospels. Thus the birth narratives are not the simple and happy presentation of Sunday school pageants. Instead, at every point there is surprise, struggle, fear, a man is speechless, common folk and even a king are afraid, people conspire to find the new born, children are slaughtered, and parents flee in the night. It is hard to read these introductions to the story of Jesus without getting hints of the resistance that is to come.

A friend of mine thinks we cannot really understand the story of Jesus because we resist the message. I think he is right and we will have to deal with it when we turn to other topics. In fact it is always a good question to ask when reading any passage: what is my resistance to the story? Sometimes the very text we are reading has the resistance in it in terms of conflict between persons, which makes it easy to identify. At other times we will simply have to ask what prevents us from hearing the message. Too often Christians read Scripture—in church and in private—without ever asking the question of resistance. This assumes we are already on God's side and are just waiting to sign up for the plan. Americans are very optimistic and also claim innocence in a naïve way. They are unlikely to ask the question of resistance. But we need to keep raising the question.

One final comment: there is a hidden message in the fact that Jesus is resisted by everyone, including his disciples and friends. The message is that if anything happens for the good in the story of Jesus, it is the work of God. It happens in spite of the confusion and fear of the disciples as well as the opposition of rulers. The coming of the Kingdom, the creation of a community of faith on earth, new life in faith, hope and love—all of these things were not created by the disciples. When all is said and done, the story of Jesus becomes a story about the God who vindicates the righteous for the sake of the redemption of the world.

5

Grace

On one of my trips up north I stopped at a grocery store. An elderly man approached a woman sitting on a bench and asked: "What are you doing?" She responded: "Waiting for Grace." To this he replied, "Grace is going around."

Grace is everywhere even though we may have trouble seeing it: daily bread, rest of the night, a beautiful day, a kind word, the joy of children, hope in the face of disappointment, or the encouragement of friends. Jesus points to the life-giving powers of God at work in the world: the rain falls on the good and the evil, the birds of the air gather their food in quiet confidence. It is in some of his parables, however, that Jesus gives us the most striking images of grace.

Consider the story of the prodigal son. A man has two sons. The youngest asks for his inheritance, receives it and goes to a far away country and squanders it. To survive he must assume the humiliating role of tending pigs. This is especially humiliating since Jews did not raise pigs for food. Something happens and the man decides to return home—after all, if he is going to do manual labor he might as well work for his father. But before he can plead his case, his father comes running out to him, receives him with open arms, and commands the servants to prepare for a celebration. The father's words still command our attention: "For this son of mine was dead and is alive again; he was lost and is found!" (Luke 15:24).

Grace

When we think about the parables, it is best to keep in mind that they are illustrations of life in the Kingdom of God. They usually offer a striking contrast to God's way of dealing with us and the way the world orders relations. In this parable, God—as represented by the father—exercises the right to treat the wayward son, not on the basis of what he deserves according to worldly standards, but on the basis of what God intends. Let us be clear: the prodigal is not an exemplary figure. Whether he was the spoiled child, or simply rebellious, in either case he turned his back on his father to pursue selfish ends. Thus the father's response is all the more surprising: instead of anger and punishment, the father restores the son to life in the family. Here is forgiveness, but more importantly, the father bestows the gifts of acceptance and love in spite of the offenses committed by the son. So it is, says Jesus, in the Kingdom of God: sinners are forgiven and given new life not on the basis of what they deserve but on the basis of God's intention to redeem the world.

The story would be straightforward and present a vivid image of familial grace even if it ended there. But Jesus knows that we are shocked and angered by the extravagance of grace. So instead of asking the listeners what they are thinking, he extends the story and places our resistance to his message into the third character in the story: the older brother. It would be an understatement to say the brother is angry. He is outraged. It would be easy to try to explain his rage by suggesting a history of rivalry and jealousy between the brothers. But that would distract from Jesus' point. Put simply, the brother speaks for conventional morality. By this I mean that his objection reflects the ordinary views of fairness and justice we use to make sense of life: people must obey general standards and rules; rewards and punishments should be based on what one does. In short, one gets what one deserves. This is simple fairness and it is the only way life makes sense and order is maintained. In games there are rules. In school, grades are based on rules and the expectation of impartial application. Social conventions and civil laws may be more complicated, but the underlying principle is the same: rewards and punishments relate to what we do. This is what I call conventional morality: status and rewards are earned and create a basis for personal identity and worth. What all this means is that the older brother is not just angry and vindictive—which he is—but he represents a very serious point of view. I regret to say that it represents much of the social order in which we live: if you do well, you are rewarded; if you fail, you are punished. You can even reverse

Part One: Origins

it: if you are blessed, you must be good; if you have hard times, you must be a failure.

There is little doubt that Jesus expands the parable because he repeatedly has encountered this restrictive mindset of conventional morality. He is criticized for associating with people who do not keep the religious practices, with shady characters like tax collectors, and even with harlots and foreigners. But Jesus has little time for conventional rules and relations of status and power. So, instead of offering an extended speech on why conventional morality is divisive and destructive, he gives us the parable of the prodigal son, with the subplot of the older brother. I am sure the parable made as many enemies as friends.

When we hear the story we have to decide whether this is a passing shot at the self-satisfied and self-righteous, or is it something more. I think it is a full frontal attack on conventional morality, which builds a fortress based on religious legalism. By this I mean that we want our relation to God to be based on our compliance with rules and regulations, what we do, and whether we have earned our way into the Kingdom. In the tradition of all the great prophets of the Old Testament, Jesus calls listeners to return to the original order of things, centered in God's grace. All of the great saving events (e.g., Exodus and the giving of the land) arose out of God's initiative. They were gifts of grace based on the divine intention to create on earth a covenant people as a light to the nations. In the right order of things, life is centered in the covenant with God: as God loves us, so we love God; as God is holy, so we are to be holy. Our holiness is not the cause of the covenant but an expression of God's new ordering of our lives. Everything is a gift of grace, even the law that sets barriers against the chaos of selfishness and violence and points us in the right direction: love God and neighbor.

Religious legalism forgets the right order of things and tries to base religion on the rules regarding what we must do to be saved. Why does it do this? For all sorts of reasons, the chief one being that these are things we can understand and control. The social order must exclude certain people and the majority needs to know they are acceptable. What we need to remember is that the impulse for religious legalism arises because people take seriously the call to holiness. You can't have self-righteousness without being concerned for righteousness. This also means the problem is not a Jewish problem but a human problem. For every example of Jewish legalism I can show you three of Christian legalism. Talk to your Catholic

Grace

friends or consider right-wing Protestantism, where rules and regulations define just about everything.

What Jesus is doing in the parable is recentering religion in the grace of God. For a moment let's play with the options. Life can be centered in ourselves, in which case we make ourselves the center of the universe. Everything revolves around us and of course we must work overtime to defend our position as perfect people. But as you know, such persons are hard to live with. Life can also be centered in some worldly authority which claims to give people status and worth. Work, family, possessions, and achievements are some of the usual suspects. The twentieth century is a graveyard of great ideologies that claimed to give persons identity and worth. But at a great and terrible price we discovered that they were idols with clay feet. And of course, there is another option, namely, living with no center. That creates confusion and even a hopelessness leading to despair. What Jesus presents is an option at the heart of Jewish faith: centering your life in the grace of God. Here one is claimed by God; here identity and worth are gifts. There is certainty allowing for trust. And there is freedom, since one does not have to make, prove, or justify oneself. In the parable, the son is given status totally based on the father's declaration. On these terms, religion is recentered; but conventional religion is decentered, or perhaps we should say, is destroyed. That is frightening to people who are comfortable trusting in their own worth and claiming that they are not sinners. It is striking that the few times Jesus displays impatience and even anger is toward those who claim righteousness based on their actions, i.e., those centered in themselves.

So what happened to the prodigal son? Did he realize that life is not to be centered in oneself, turn around, and take responsibility for his life, honoring and loving his father? And did the older brother get the point, realize that he had been going through the motions, angry at his father and brother, and in a very different kind of way, repent his arrogance? Jesus does not tell us. He likes narratives but does not expand on these brief stories. But he draws us into the story. Which character do you identify with? Are you the wise, gracious father, unswerving in the desire to reclaim the lost? Or are you the older brother, feeling under recognized, but taking comfort in the fact that you are superior to the disobedient child? Or does the parable draw you into a new narrative for your life: that you have been lost, wandering around trying all sorts of things, but suddenly have been given life as a gift of grace? Christian teaching, preaching, hymns, art, and symbols overflow with images of grace because that is the doorway into new life. There still is a lot of the older brother in ourselves, family members, churches, and the society proposing that we center our lives in do-able things. But every now and then the parable shatters our confidence in such things and calls us to center our lives in the grace of God.

6

Justice

IF GRACE IS THE point of origin, where does it lead? Since grace is an activity of God, it can not be plucked out of the story and made into an isolated value. What God does is always part of the divine plan that Jesus names the Kingdom of God. The grace directed toward the lost son inevitably leads to the recentering of the community. That is, grace leads to what we call justice. I put it that way because in the Gospels the word *justice* does not appear. But of course it is in the background of many teachings and parables of Jesus. I want to use the word because we use it to describe the relations between people. It also serves as a mark of the healthy community.

Whenever my pastor father preached on the parable of the laborers in the vineyard there would be a big argument at the Sunday dinner table. This is the parable where Jesus says—and note carefully—that the Kingdom of heaven is like a man who hired workers at different times of the day to work in his vineyard (Matt 20:1–16). But when he paid them at the end of the day, he gave them all the same wage. Then those who had started early in the morning were angry that those who started in mid-afternoon received the same wages for much less work. The owner's response to those who had worked all day is that he paid them exactly what he promised them.

Well, you can imagine the argument at the table, where everyone—three kids, mother, grandmother, and Aunt Hattie—let father know that that was the most unfair thing we had ever heard. For us kids, the thought of someone getting the same pay for doing less work was so unfair that it was intolerable. Your grandfather loved it because he liked riddles. For him the parable was a riddle. Even though it confused and aroused passions, he liked telling the punchline. Actually, the punchline is at the beginning: "The Kingdom of heaven is like . . ." No, the parable is not about labor relations in factories, teachers' wage scales, or even pay to kids for Saturday chores. The world has worked out all sorts of ways to settle those matters, some being fair and others being grossly unfair. But in the Kingdom of God, where God recenters all relations between God and persons, God will claim all with the same grace. If grace gives life, justice is the will to give life to all. When God gives life, loves, accepts, forgives, or sustains, there are no gradations, no half or quarter payments, no first and second class gifts. Justice wills to restore the entire community.

This is, of course, a hard pill to swallow. We want the Kingdom, or religion, to be run according to the same rules we have devised to run the world. That allows us to control even God's Kingdom by our standards. And of course, we want to come into the Kingdom with all of our status, privilege, power, and wealth. After all, we earned it. Consider the rich man who will not give up his wealth in order to enter the Kingdom of God. He wants both and will not accept Jesus' terms for entrance, namely to renounce his claims to worldly things. If you get this point, then you can understand why we are so quick to turn a religion of grace into a legalism based on conventional morality. And we can also say, if you were disturbed by the parable of the prodigal son, the parable of the laborers is really outrageous. But Jesus is deconstructing or decentering our well defined world of rules and merit. Justice has less to do with rewarding and punishing people and more to do with all people being restored to life in the community.

This parable of the laborers provokes the resistance people have to Jesus. We need to remember that much of this comes from what we would call good people, that is, people who believe in God and keep their faith by moral and religious practices. They are not thieves and robbers, they have kept their marriage vows, they don't associate with shady characters like tax collectors or women with bad reputations. They also keep the religious observances and holidays, as well as the social and dietary rules. These things are important because they define faithfulness to the covenant. So when Jesus associates with the so-called public sinners and foreigners, or is willing to heal (i.e., work) on the Sabbath, they are shocked.

It is the equivalent of paying all the workers the same thing, when it is obvious that they don't all deserve the same thing. Notice we are back to the question: what do we deserve? Jesus' answer is that we have already been receiving more than we deserve (from parents, friends, and God). Furthermore, in the Kingdom of God what we receive will be determined completely by God according to the divine plan to restore the lost and heal the community.

Which brings us back to the question of justice. It is easy to talk about grace because most people want love and acceptance. The announcement of unconditional love to me is great news. But justice is a hard sell. Americans are much more interested in liberty and would gladly forget the "justice for all" part. Justice has to do with the other guy, who could be the brother I don't like or even some guy I don't even know. So why should I be interested in him? In the Bible there are several classic ways of answering this question: One is to affirm that God created us all and cares for all as a father cares for his children. So, if we are all sons and daughters of God, then we are brothers and sisters and are bound by the same obligation to care for one another. A second approach is to remember the Mosaic covenant: God is holy and expects the people of the covenant to be holy. This means that the social interactions between us (i.e., issues of justice) are crucial. A third approach is simply to go right to the commandment: love God and love your neighbor. Jesus formulates his version of this based on verses in the Old Testament. Elsewhere, there are variations: for example, if you say you love God but hate your brother, then you are a liar. The point being: one cannot love God without loving your neighbor.

So you can see that the question of justice keeps coming up because it is essentially tied both to who God is as well as how we are to treat one another. What I find striking—and unfortunately it is too often not discussed—is the connection between grace and justice in the teaching of Jesus. Sometimes the connection is lost because the teaching is so brief and takes the form of a command. For example, take the command to love your enemies in Matthew 5:44. (We could also use the commands to be reconciled to your brother, or to share your coat, or to walk the second mile.) This command is so unusual it takes us back and we are not sure what to do. Since Jesus gives it, we are reluctant to object, but we wonder where he gets this idea. The distinction between friends and enemies is part of an ordered society based on rules and our interests—

which enemies have violated. The desire for revenge reflects the desire for punishment and/or compensation when we have been wronged. For good reason the story of the father's unconditional love toward his rebellious son gets more attention than this verse about loving our enemies. The one relates to grace given to individuals, the other relates to a change in social practice toward others.

I think Jesus stakes everything on the connection between grace and justice. To whom is grace given? To those who have broken trust with God and neighbor, those who have betrayed others, those who have broken the law. Grace is for people who have committed real sins—not silly things—and now live in disgrace. At every point in the Bible where God creates a covenant, God forgives, calls, or anoints. Grace accepts unworthy people and brings them into the healing power of God. In our love of the wrong things, our turning away and living our own lives, we have become enemies of God. The coming of the Kingdom does not mean an apocalyptic end of the world, but a restoration wherein God makes right what has been broken. So now the punchline: If God can be gracious to each of us, then we are called to be gracious to those who have sinned against us (those we have classified as our enemies).

What begins in grace is completed in new relations with others (justice). In this light, the teachings of Jesus in the Sermon on the Mount only make sense if we take up a position of life in the Kingdom of God. In the new realm inaugurated by God's grace, the members shall be expected and empowered to practice a new righteousness: they shall seek to be reconciled to those who offend them, avoid the ill will and selfishness that create violence and sexual abuse, turn the other cheek and go the second mile. They shall break conventional rules and love their enemies, practice giving without any reward, and avoid creating treasures on earth. They shall hold back on judging others and instead seek to produce the harvest of faithful service. Such people shall be quick and content to call upon God in the words: "Our Father . . ." Such people shall be called blessed because they hunger and thirst for righteousness, are merciful, and make peace (see Matt 5–7). In the Kingdom defined by God's justice, people are expected and empowered to act in new ways reflecting God's intention for the community.

But the disciples don't get it. James and John, brothers, listen to all this and still ask whether they can have positions of power when the Kingdom comes. They want to do to those in power what the powerful have been doing to them for years and years. If Jesus wants to turn the tables by recentering religion in its well-spring of grace, they want to turn the tables on the powerful by lording over others. To this Jesus responds: "But it shall not be so among you . . ." (Mark 10:43).

There is an ethic of justice in Jesus' teachings but it is not like conventional wisdom. It has to do with grace freely given and the healing of our hearts and minds. It goes directly to the new relations between people, who seek to share, be reconciled, and make peace—just as they have received such gifts from God.

7

Compassion

HERE IS ANOTHER PARABLE of Jesus. A man travels from Jerusalem down to Jericho, in the Jordan River valley. But he is robbed and beaten, then left to die. A priest comes upon the scene, but makes it quite clear that he wants nothing to do with this wounded man: he "passed by on the other side." Then a Levite (a specific group of priests) also sees the man. But he too "passed by on the other side." A third man arrives on the scene, and in marked contrast to the other two, comes near to the man, sees him and has compassion on him. But he is a Samaritan. Now Samaritans trace their origin to ancient Israel but are not considered legitimate by official Judaism. So, the hero of the parable, the one who shows mercy, is one generally treated as a despised foreigner. It is the Samaritan who cleans the man's wounds with wine and oil, places him on his donkey, takes him to an inn and makes arrangements for his care. It is this man who turns out to be the good neighbor.

For all its simplicity, this is a very complicated story. It is loaded with social criticism, first directed at the religious establishment and then at religious-cultural prejudice. The two members of the priesthood walk by and leave the man in pain. Are they so preoccupied with their own schedules, duties, and rules that they are unable to show mercy? It is not clear whether they do fear being made unclean by contact with open wounds, or whether they are afraid of the robbers. Fear does strange things to us. Jesus makes it clear that their walking by was not an accident, as each deliberately "passed by on the other side." How sad it is when those who should see clearly the central message of religion miss a chance to show us what it is all about. We do not have to look very far to find examples today in the religious establishment.

But the story is even more disturbing. The hero of the story turns out to be a despised Samaritan. There is probably an element of irony here: Jews don't associate with Samaritans because they are impure, but the Samaritan touches the unclean, wounded man in order to show compassion. To name him the Good Samaritan is to reject the walls of alienation between Jews and Samaritans and pose the question: just what is true religion?

A final complication, seldom noted, is that the parable does not really answer the question posed. How strange that one of Jesus' greatest parables changes the subject. Why is this? The scene begins when a lawyer (i.e., someone versed in religious and civil law) asks what one must do to be saved. Jesus responds by asking him what the law says. The lawyer replies: Love God and neighbor. So Jesus agrees and tells him to do it. But the lawyer wants to get technical and asks: Who is my neighbor? That is the subject put to Jesus before a crowd of listeners. It is in this context that Jesus tells the parable of the Good Samaritan. To make it very clear that he is not answering the question, Jesus concludes the parable with this question: "Which of these three do you think was a neighbor to the man who fell into the hands of the robbers." The lawyer responds: "The one who showed him mercy." Again Jesus says: Do it (Luke 10:36–37).

So what lies behind Jesus' refusal to answer the question: Who is my neighbor? I do not think this is a minor or technical issue. Jesus refuses to answer it because it sidetracks the command to love God and neighbor. It sidetracks the discussion by placing us in a controlling position. By defining who is my neighbor, I also get to say who is not my neighbor! Once this is established, we can set up rules regarding when and how I should help my neighbor in specific situations—all codified in regulations so we are feeling good that we have loved God and neighbor. So I think Jesus' refusal to answer this question is his rejection of the elaborate system of setting rules for what we should or should not do, and how we earn rewards or punishments. God has created all human beings and all are my neighbors. Now if you say that is an intolerable burden, you are correct. But Jesus would rather have us worry about that than feel comfortable knowing that we have cared for the officially recognized neighbors. There

Part One: Origins

is no easy answer to how and when we should love God and neighbor. Now back to the parable.

Compassion is the key to the parable. Now compassion is much more than pity or feeling sorry for someone. Nearly every day we see photos of adults and children in terrible situations. We shudder at the sight of such suffering. But we move on to other stories and do nothing. By contrast, compassion is a bond we affirm with other persons, born of their suffering. As the word's origin suggests, it is a form of co-suffering. Compassion causes us to place ourselves with another and take appropriate action. This is what it means to love the neighbor, i.e., to be willing to share in his or her suffering. So we have to ask: Why would anyone do that? To answer this we need to make some connections. Compassion is created by grace, which gives life to us and which we are willing to share. As grace gives new life, so it also empowers the receiver to give life. In this sense, compassion is not an isolated personal virtue which some have and others don't. Compassion is the instrument of justice derived from grace received. We deal justly with others by standing with them in their need as brothers and sisters.

As you can imagine, we need to deal with our resistance to compassion. Why is compassion so hard and even threatening? The parable suggests the problem may lie in our fear. To stand with others in their suffering can place one in uncomfortable and even dangerous situations. There are many modern-day versions of defilement—loss of social status or the potential for contracting illness. In our time some of the greatest examples of compassion come from persons who freely worked with those suffering from disease. As a child I was always amazed by pictures of Albert Schweitzer working with Africans in his clinic where people suffered from contagious diseases. Perhaps you had that reaction to seeing photos of Mother Teresa in India. Their freedom to show compassion is astounding and reveals how much we are bound by fear.

But I think there is another reason in our time why there is so little compassion. It is the prevalent economic and moral legalism. Let me explain. On the one hand we have increasingly reduced the connections between ourselves and other people, especially people of different color and class. It is acceptable to deny that there are any common bonds. One brand of economics has promulgated the dogma that the sole purpose of corporations is making money for stockholders. Away with social responsibility! Appeals to the common good are met with such anger that one is overwhelmed by how strong the divisions in our society have become. As a result, the concept of neighbor has no meaning, which means there is no place for compassion. On the other hand, the motivation for compassion is undercut by a legalism that tells us people in need do not deserve the benefits of modern society. What rankles is the thought that someone is getting something for nothing, i.e., they did not earn it as we did. In effect we have moved away from the older Protestant gratitude to God for undeserved gifts freely given, to a quite harsh confidence that what we have, we have earned by our own hands. Thus the great divide is created between those who earn the benefits of our society and those who don't. And if you have not earned them, then you don't deserve them.

What makes this kind of economic-moral legalism objectionable is that it overlooks the extent to which the successful ones have in fact received freely from previous generations, parents, friends, teachers, benefactors, and, of all sources, the government! The myth of the self-made man is indeed a myth, with disastrous consequences because of its inherent self-righteousness. The legalism also overlooks the extent to which the benefits bestowed on the haves were in fact the result of violence and exploitation of people and nature. It is for good reason that those who support this legalism must rewrite American history so that the conquest of the land over its original inhabitants, slavery, exploitation of miners, factory workers, child labor, and subordination of women must all be ignored. (Just a bit of local history: in the town of Ely, Minnesota, during an 80-year period, over 260 miners died. These men produced some of the iron ore which changed America. Did their families ever receive compensation for their loss? Who benefited from such losses?)

I don't think it is stretching things to draw connections between the three parables we have discussed so far: the prodigal son, laborers in the vineyard, and the good Samaritan. Each parable is about grace and each parable evokes great resistance. In the first, the older brother objects to the welcome for his brother because he does not deserve it. In the second, the early laborers object to the reward system because some don't seem to deserve it. In the third, the wounded man is ignored because he does not deserve our time or the exposure to danger which might be incurred. Each parable tells the story of how someone is empowered to cross barriers that divide in order to restore life. In each case, grace creates a new community of the lost, the excluded, and the wounded. Jesus calls the grace of the Samaritan compassion: the willingness to recognize the stranger as a member of the human family and share his or her suffering.

We have, unfortunately, labeled compassion as an individual virtue which some possess for strange reasons. (Perhaps that makes it easier to ignore Mother Teresa.) It is also the case with charity, i.e., the act of giving small amounts to publicized causes out of pity. Thus we keep at arm's length the underlying issue of compassion, namely, that we are bound together in a common life. In the Old Testament, the prophets will not let the rich and powerful forget this. Frequently the means they use is to ask about widows and orphans. At the time, women were totally dependent for status and life upon husbands, and children on fathers. Therefore, widows and orphans find themselves without any protector or safety net. They are at the mercy of a society quite self-content with its success and luxury. If one looks on them with the kind of economic self-righteousness just mentioned, they don't deserve our help. So, the prophets like to ask the wealthy society which also claims to be good, what have you done lately for widows and orphans? The question is a judgment against their self-righteous disregard of the poor, it is also a reminder that they have forgotten that they were once poor and that they have received what they have by God's mercy. Jesus does not refer to the prophets on this point, but I am sure their demand for justice is in the background when he tells the parable of compassion.

8

Faith

THE QUESTION OF FAITH keeps coming up in the story of Jesus. But it is not our concern whether God exists, nor faith in the sense of believing lots of stuff. It definitely does not mean what is often said, namely, that faith is believing something without reason or evidence. Rather, in the Gospels, faith has to do with whether we trust God. I suppose we might say, speaking colloquially, it has to do with: Who do you trust?

Trust and the Temptations of this World

The temptations of Jesus in Matthew and Luke are helpful at this point. But first we need a word regarding the origin of this material. Mark tells us Jesus was tempted but gives no details. So where did Matthew and Luke get the long versions, since Jesus was alone? Either Jesus told his disciples of his experience or the account reflects their interpretation of the struggle the disciples perceived going on in Jesus. It was obvious Jesus had gifts of wisdom and power to teach and heal. Thus it is quite natural to assume he would be tempted, just as they were, to abuse his gifts and betray his mission. Other passages make it clear that the temptation to forsake his mission was an ongoing issue. For these reasons I have no trouble with the narratives as reflections from his followers. They saw clearly that Jesus was tempted, just as they were.

The long versions are very carefully constructed and layered with meanings. In Luke the second and third temptations are reversed from the order in Matthew, but there is no special meaning to that. At the simplest level, the three temptations are: turn stones into bread, leap from the temple (i.e., to see if God's angels will catch him), and finally, bow down and worship Satan and gain all of the kingdoms of this world. All three have to do with power and its use. Many a sermon has portrayed how Jesus was tempted to use his power for monetary gain, dazzle everyone by leaping from the temple to prove his special status, and to give allegiance to Satan in exchange for worldly splendor. When we approach the temptations in this way, the emphasis falls upon the temptation of worldly things. And of course, Jesus refuses to do these things.

At this initial level, therefore, the temptations present a sharp contrast between what the world might offer and loyalty to God. The issue is thus framed in kind of an either/or: the world or God. I regret to say that many Christians have jumped at this, assuming that things of this world must be shunned in favor of the religious life. The obvious form of this is the monastic life, which affirms celibacy, and practices a simple life with varying degrees of isolation from the larger society. The great St. Augustine was so in love with the world and its pleasures that he delayed and delayed his baptism because for him becoming a Christian meant a complete rejection of the world. You will appreciate one line from his autobiographical work where he declares how much he wanted to take the step, "but not now." There is no doubt that the temptations of Jesus involve a choice between God and the world. As noted, the one temptation is more than a preoccupation with the world but allegiance to Satan.

A somewhat different light is shed on the matter when we examine what Jesus actually says to Satan. I want you to look at these responses because they clarify the nature of faith. In each case, Jesus quotes portions of verses from the Book of Deuteronomy in the Old Testament.

- Regarding turning stones to bread: "One does not live by bread alone, but by every word that comes from the mouth of God."
- Regarding a leap from the temple: "Do not put the Lord your God to the test."
- Regarding allegiance to Satan: "Worship the Lord your God, and serve only him."

Now, when we think of the temptations from the standpoint of how Jesus responds—not how we interpret them—it is clear that the emphasis falls

Faith

on trust in God, not the attractive powers of the world. Each temptation asks Jesus to betray his trust in God. I don't think this is quibbling or a matter of six of one and a half dozen of another. We end up with a very different view of faith and the Christian life when we follow out this approach to the temptations.

Here in summary form is Jesus' response to the three temptations: In the first, he dares not become totally preoccupied with worldly things but must be centered in the Word which comes from God. There is no question of needing some bread. In the second, he refuses to make demands of God or try to maneuver God into a situation where God is forced to prove that God loves him. Here an historical note is important: the full verse in Deuteronomy refers to an incident in the wilderness during Israel's flight from Egypt to Canaan. There the people demanded that God provide food and water to prove God's faithfulness. God complies but warns them, don't do that again. It is an unusual response on the part of the Almighty, more like that of many a parent. But the point is that God is God and not the wonder-working deity of popular religion. Finally, in the third response, Jesus sees the issue quite clearly as the worship (i.e., trust) of God alone. You cannot have it both ways: the worship of Satan (and worldly things) and the worship of God.

When we read with care the original verses Jesus is using from the Book of Deuteronomy, the emphasis falls on faith as trust in God:

- In this world one must have bread, but life cannot be centered in bread (i.e., worldly needs and goods) alone. To do so is to turn from God because we no longer trust God to provide what we really need for the good life.
- In this world there will be many occasions when we wonder if God really is present, sustaining us with loving kindness. To demand that God prove God's love is a betrayal of trust. How would you feel if your child or spouse said to you: If you love me, do this?
- In this world we are to participate in and enjoy all the things the creation offers, but worship as the ultimate trust and commitment of our hearts and minds is to be given to God alone. We can break trust with God by conspiring with the devil in our pursuit of all the splendors of the world, or we can simply make the splendors of the world our ultimate goal. In either case, God is no longer the center of our ultimate trust.

Part One: Origins

Beyond Either/Or

When we place the emphasis on faith as trust in God, we have the option of incorporating into that trust our life in the world—a life which God has given us. In the case of Jesus, this plays out as to whether the one anointed by the Spirit and gifted with power will betray God's trust in him. When the Gospel writers use the phrase, "he set his face toward Jerusalem," they clearly are conscious of the intentional decision Jesus made to be faithful to his mission. He will not be tempted by the world or Satan, nor by fear of the consequences of proclaiming the Kingdom of God. What all this means is that for Jesus, faith in God does not draw him out of the world but into the world entangled in misguided and false trust, where faith in God has been betrayed in so many ways. I find it striking that in fulfilling his task, he engages in table fellowship (i.e., breaks bread and drinks wine) as well as lives among people in their daily tasks.

So how would this view of faith play out for us? Several passages of Scripture come to mind. The first is an aspect of the creation story in Genesis 2. In this story the male is created first and set in the garden with everything he needs. But he is lonely and God makes a helper or partner for him. They are to live together, love and work, and trust the God who has created them. The thing that interests me is that God does not take offense at the man's dissatisfaction with being alone. He does have all he needs in the garden and, most important, he has God. By creating the woman, God creates a triangle, where God is easily the unnecessary third party. But here is the point: God does not treat this request like a jilted lover. It is God's intention for human beings to find pleasure in one another, to love and work in the world God has created. What we have in this story is not an either/or of world or God, but the inclusion of the world in our lives, centered in trust in God.

The disappointing news is that St. Augustine makes a brief reference to this option. He suggests that since God has created all things and they are good, we are to love things *in God.* But this proves to be the road not taken by him. Instead of exploring what that might mean regarding the relation of love between two persons, work, or possessing things of this world, he takes the other road toward the monastic option where it is the world vs. God.

The second passage I want to call to your attention is in the Sermon on the Mount. Indeed, Augustine might well claim it to support his option. But I think it goes the other way, in spite of the initial choice set before the listeners at the beginning. When we get to the end of the discourse, I think Jesus makes clear that faith is not a matter of choosing God instead of the world, but finding the appropriate way to trust God in the midst of the tensions of this world. Here is the opening line to Matthew 6:24–34:

> No one can serve two masters, for a slave will either hate the one
> and love the other, or be devoted to the one and despise the other.
> You cannot serve God and wealth.

At the outset it would appear that an absolute division is being made between God and things of this world. But we need to ask what is meant by *serve*. It is fair to assume that serve in this context does not mean engaging in work or making other limited commitments. In this context serve refers to ultimate loyalty, aligning all time and effort toward one goal, and placing the highest degree of love and trust in one person or object. Such service cannot be divided between two masters, since the obligations conflict and it is impossible to serve rightly each master. Note that Jesus offers the warning about serving two masters with the subject of wealth in mind. To make wealth the absolute object of one's loyalty excludes service to God.

But does service to God exclude all forms of loyalty to the world? We find ourselves with varying degrees of obligation and loyalty to parents, spouse, children, siblings, neighbors, friends, work, nation, and many other commitments. Since God has created us for life in this complex set of loyalties, I assume that we are called to find some way of solving the challenge. Human beings vary in the ways they resolve the tensions and conflicts between these many loyalties. God can be excluded in almost an infinite number of ways. So the question becomes: What wisdom is Jesus giving us to resolve the problem?

I think when faced with a hard issue, it is best to go back to what we know for sure, namely, Jesus' proclamation of the coming of the Kingdom. Jesus is calling us to recenter our lives in the new community of God. But how can we make such a switch in orientation given the requirements and threats facing us at every turn? The answer is given in the next verse: "Do not be anxious . . ." (or as a newer translation reads: "Do not worry about your life . . .") The reason we are anxious is that we don't trust God. We fear that if we turn toward a life governed by the Kingdom ethos we will not have enough food, clothes, and other necessities. After reminding the listeners of how God cares for the birds of the air and the flowers of the field, he assures them that their heavenly Father knows what they need. Then, to pull it all together, Jesus declares: "But strive first for the kingdom of God and his righteousness, and all these things will be given to you as well." Again it is not a question of denying our worldly needs but placing them in the proper order to our ultimate trust and confidence in God. Faith as trust is the confidence that God will fulfill promises made to us for life—genuine human life on earth under the rule of God. From this perspective, faith does not draw us out of the world or deny our human needs, but rather gathers them together into our life marked by trust in God.

In another verse in the Sermon on the Mount, Jesus offers a critique of life preoccupied with worldly treasures. The problem, he says, with such preoccupation is that "where your treasure is, there your heart will be also" (Matt 6:21). In this light, the opposite of trust in God is trusting in worldly things. This is the equivalent of serving the other master, it is what stands behind the three temptations, and it is our human attempt to conquer all worries. But as Jesus reminds the listeners, treasures on earth decay or can be stolen. Even more important, they turn us from the true life found in the love of God and neighbor.

Second Thoughts

To this point I have spoken of faith as trusting God while living in the world. No doubt this approach annoys some because it appears to put the cart before the horse: we are asked to trust God before we know that God exists. I would agree that this is not the usual approach in what is called an Introduction to Religion (or Philosophy of Religion). So let's admit what is going on. First, I have not discussed the so-called proofs for God's existence because I side with those who don't think they work. They try to move from the need for a first cause, a Designer, or the Highest Being to the existence of such. Second, when that does not work, writers often turn to a general discussion about the human condition, suggesting that we might find glimpses or points of contact between our lives and God. I admire such writings because they raise the question of God and lead us to the point of making a decision. But too often we are left in the narthex wondering if we should enter the sanctuary; in fact, living in the narthex and thinking about the issues and arguments can become a way of life.

I have not taken either of these two approaches, partly because they offer limited help in finding God, but partly because of the way they pose the question. They tend to assume that we are free, rational thinkers, existing in a world without any commitments, asking whether we should believe in a god. That may describe some people who have practiced a discipline of critical thinking and intellectual freedom. But that is not the general human condition. It is for this reason I take a different approach. As H. Richard Niebuhr argued, most people already practice a variety of forms of trust and loyalty in their personal and family life. They also express commitments as members of communities in their social and political life. This perspective is not new. For example, Augustine illustrated that we are primarily creatures of love and that our love motivates mind and will. In a similar vein, Luther was fond of saying that faith of the heart is either directed toward God or idol. We are never neutral but are constantly giving our hearts away. Luther's comment takes us back to Jesus' declaration about the tensions inherent in serving two masters. I take this as a starting place and think it is helpful to explore these tensions.

As already noted my approach does not offer arguments to justify faith, but assumes we are already knee deep in acts of trust and loyalty. This does not automatically lead to faith in the one, true God, but it creates the context for such faith. When we are brought to such faith, it is not by arguments but by a crisis: we discover that what we trusted failed us; the safe world, so carefully constructed of values we trusted, suddenly fell apart. I remember speaking to a neighbor in my backyard the day after Nixon resigned. He was devastated. That fortified world of DuPage County conservative values had been demolished. For years they had prided themselves in not living in Democratic Cook County! It was a crisis of major proportions.

When such a crisis occurs, we find ourselves in a vulnerable state, faced with several options: like a jilted lover we can swear off any kind of trust; we can turn quickly to something else; we can despair; or we face the possibility of trust in the God who offers a new way of being in the world. What is characteristic of this transformative moment for Jews and Christians is that the God we turn to ends up being the One who has destroyed our false faith. In this sense, these moments of crisis involve a double discovery: we discover what we believed about gods or God is

Part One: Origins

transformed into a new form of trust; we discover what we knew about ourselves is also transformed from a false sense of self to a new identity centered in the God who gives life. A quick reference back to the parable of the prodigal son illustrates the point: God proves not to be the legalistic, vindictive God who punishes sinners, but the one who gives life to the undeserving; we find ourselves no longer able to think of ourselves as the law-abiding, deserving son or daughter, but as the prodigal who stands before God in total need. (A variation on this is that we find ourselves in the role of the older brother, demanding punishment for sinners and assuming that we are sinless.)

Now to take this one step further, Christians are people whose faith has been formed in this double way by the story of Jesus. Just about any part of the story may become the occasion for a shattering of our confidence in our current world or the possibility of having life open to new forms of grace. For example, the announcement of the coming of the Kingdom of God, or parables of God's wondrous grace, or teachings which call us to recenter our lives in God's will—these parts of the story can so easily function in a twofold way. They expose the limited and divisive way we have thought about God and other people, and they become the invitation to participate in new life. But consider this: if any one of these parts of the story can both shatter and give new life, consider how the final sequence of Jesus' death and God's response have such potential for giving birth to faith. In his death we are reminded of the suffering of the innocent for righteousness' sake; in his resurrection we are reminded of God's faithfulness to those who suffer and God's will to redeem the world. In these ways Jesus' story becomes the occasion for the transformation of our resistance and our limited beliefs into the trust of the God who wills life for sinners. Perhaps this explains why, upon announcing the coming of the Kingdom of God in Mark 1:14, the first thing Jesus says is: Repent. We cannot believe unless we first acknowledge that we have trusted the wrong things.

One way of understanding the approach I am taking is to recognize that for Jews and Christians, the knowledge of God is a moral act. It has a certain logic, but it also involves what we love and hold most dear. Faith is not something we can discuss in a neutral, dispassionate way, as if nothing were at stake. To know God is to have to choose between giving God our ultimate love and loyalty, or directing them elsewhere. This is why the prophets of the Old Testament equate knowing God with loving

God and one's neighbor. It is also why in one tradition, being faithful is remembering who God is and what God has done. The opposite of faith is not disbelief but forgetting. It is in forgetfulness that we are willing to create a false view of ourselves and the world around us (for example, that we have created everything, fully deserve what we have, and owe no one anything).

These second thoughts on faith are offered just to let you know that there is a rationale behind my refusal to try to make a case for God before we talk about anything else. I am more inclined to propose you read the history of the twentieth century and look at the idols the nations have created, the evil done on our behalf, and the ways we try to avoid an honest assessment of our own history. It is in the face of all the violence and suffering, along with the naïveté and hypocrisy, that the words of the prophets and the story of Jesus give insight into what it means to have faith in God.

9

Light

FOR THE BIBLE, LIGHT shines in two directions: toward knowledge and moral goodness. Surrounding each of these heavy-weight topics are two questions: What is the light? and Who has the light? If you have it or know where it is, then you have access to knowledge and goodness. This sets you apart, elevates you, and gives you access to power. But there have always been huge debates over who has the light.

When I was in graduate school, the culture was uncomfortable with questions of ultimate value and moral goodness. Such topics were increasingly being relegated to the private life and deemed inappropriate for public discussion. In the public realm, issues were supposed to be resolved by analysis and control—what we call science and technology. This approach claimed credibility because of the success of the modern, Western world. But the last fifty years have demonstrated that there are many issues not resolved by analysis and control, be they religious, moral, or cultural. We now seem to be more open to these questions of value. During the Cold War, East and West argued over which side saw the true light regarding economic theory and the course of history. In this country, politics and economics are deeply involved in debates over the environment, civil rights, women's rights, and questions of equity regarding pay and benefits. As I write this, there are debates going on in northern Minnesota whether or not lakes and woods can survive new, large scale mining operations. Twenty-five years ago Ronald Reagan declared that government is evil and the Tea Party now boldly leads a charge based

Light

on that premise. Terrorism and warfare between Christians and Muslims have made it impossible to ignore the religious history of Europe and the Middle East. So, questions about ultimate values and the purpose of worldly knowledge have become center stage, whether we are prepared for them or not.

Most Christians claim to have seen the light, but usually with some caution and qualifications. Yes, there is light in this world and one can even affirm that we have it, but it is a gift and something we do not control. It is not in us and we are not its source. But not all would agree with this modest affirmation. For example, some have always wanted to argue that there is a direct connection between our reason or moral sensitivities and the true light. So you can find so-called arguments to prove God's existence, based on the assumption that we can construct sentences together in a logical pattern which will obligate us to conclude that God exists. Or, if you go to a bookstore and browse the current best-sellers you can find books claiming that the true light of religion is in you. Very often this idea is gift wrapped in an attractive appeal: it is suggested that the light in us has been suppressed by organized religion. The argument usually includes a rejection of various doctrines (original sin, revelation, authority of Scripture, or the Trinity), claiming that these ideas have been used to control the true light and prevent ordinary folk from access to it. By appealing to the anger among people toward the institutional church and its male leaders, the claim that the light is in each of us quickly connects with long-standing anger against church officials.

This highly charged situation requires that we do some digging as to why most Christians are cautious about claiming the light is in us. To speak in broad strokes, it comes down to two issues: first, Jews and Christians make a serious distinction between God and human beings, and second, human beings have a tendency to substitute their own light for God's. Let's take them one at a time.

Christians affirm a very positive view of human life, based on the Genesis affirmation that God created the world and it is good. In one stroke this excludes any view that suggests that, if there are problems, they exist because the world was created that way. In its essential form, life is good. But—and this is the tricky part—human life is finite, that is, not divine. We are made of the stuff of earth and return to earth. Thus human existence is a peculiar combination: made of physical stuff of the earth and related to other forms of life, it possesses a mysterious power capable of love and creative activity. We are able to possess the light of knowledge and goodness, but we are not the source of such light. If you ask, How can we have the light of God if finite humans are not divine?, Jews and Christians answer this by saying: God uses things of this world to reveal the divine purpose. Though created of finite stuff, we are also created in the image of God. We are spirit-filled creatures capable of personal relations with one another and God. This role as receivers rather than creators of ultimate light is expressed in the two great verses: "In thy light we shall see light" and "The Lord is my light and my salvation."

Thus, Jews look to covenants made with Abraham, Moses, and David. They celebrate the light revealed in the experience of Exodus and the giving of the Torah, which includes the Ten Commandments. They listen to the words of prophets who dare to speak for God, knowing that they are not always the best transmitters of the light. Christians say yes to all of this and also look to the story of Jesus: to teachings, signs and wonders, and his life of fidelity to the Kingdom. In effect, Christians affirm with the Gospel of John that the divine light shines in this world in Jesus Christ (John 1:1–14).

Now let's complicate things. We started with one theme that affirms caution because there is a difference between God and human beings. The second theme prompts more than caution, but rather strong opposition to any claim that we possess or create the light. I am referring to the basic recognition that what we claim to be the light is usually limited and impartial. Sometimes the problem is simply the limitations of our context, at other times it is that our vision has been blurred by personal and/or group self-interests. How does one explain that the Founding Fathers conceived of a new political order based on liberty but then excluded women and wrote into the Constitution the right to own slaves? How easy it is for us to see the falsehoods in the claims of dictators such as Stalin, but then resist the limits and impartiality in our own claims to truth and moral goodness. In the rhetorical warfare of our current political situation, both sides use arguments to wound the other without much regard for whether they themselves could withstand such an assault. In terms of matters of the heart, human beings seem to be capable of the most callous disregard for promises they have made, but quite enterprising in the way amorous relations are rationalized.

Christians have traditionally explained this by holding that the human will and reason are corruptible, capable of all manner of selfishness and evil. One writer reminds us that every war has been justified as a cause of self-defense or the pursuit of noble values. A well known prayer asks for forgiveness for the evil done on our behalf—implying that we willingly allow others to do things which bring benefits to us. In a recent trial of a financial adviser who swindled his investors, the man struck a plea with the prosecutor and the judge. But to gain the lesser sentence he had to stand in court and say: "I knowingly and willingly defrauded these people." Such moments of honesty are rare. But even more important, we resist the implications of such honesty because of what it says about us. We are reluctant to admit that reasonable, educated people would violate moral trust. We still harbor the old liberal assumption that only the poor or scoundrels from the wrong side of the tracks do bad things. Later we will talk some more about the implications of so-called good people doing bad things. But here the point is that humans are prone to selfishness, which infects our vision of the truth and our estimation of what is good. So, all this creates the second level of caution regarding any claim to knowing all there is on a subject or possessing perfect goodness in a contested situation.

I need to add an important note at this point, because it has huge implications for all sorts of things. Finitude is not the same as sin. We are not sinful because we are finite. That would suggest a necessity or determinism built into the creation, namely, that because we are finite therefore we are doomed to selfishness and idolatry. But at the same time we do have to recognize that finitude has limitations. We are born into a specific time and place, soak up that culture and language, and become immersed in the concerns and fears of our family and social network. To the extent that we take our context as the only source of light, then the circumstances of our birth begin to merge with idolatry. To the extent that we develop our likes and dislikes based on our loves and hatreds, then finitude and selfishness become so intertwined that it is difficult to think of them as separate. Did the Germans and Austrians hate the Jews only in the 1930s, or was it a sickness that had infected their culture and the entire west for centuries? More illustrations will be offered later. For now the point is that finitude and sin are not the same, though it is often difficult to distinguish them.

Given all this caution, and even downright suspicion, we are faced with an obvious question: How can Christians claim to possess the light? No matter how clear or pure it is upon the giving, how can the gift of light remain clear or pure in the hands of finite and sinful human beings? Let me answer the question by going directly to that wonderful saying of Jesus: "You are the light of the world." There is not much caution or suspicion here. So how are we going to answer the question in light of Jesus' declaration?

Let's begin by accepting the saying of Jesus and not trying to duck the problem with an appeal to some technicality in the writing of the Gospels. What is it about Jesus' followers that sets them apart from everyone else to such a degree that they possess the key for truth and goodness? It would be fair to assume that it is not something they had before they met Jesus. They came from diverse backgrounds and places and were not markedly different from most of the people Jesus encounters in his travels. That leaves us with the option that they are set apart because of something happening to them in the coming of Jesus. Or, to put it in terms of his teaching, they are the light of the world because they have heard and accepted the declaration of the coming of the Kingdom of God. In other words, they possess the light not because it was already in them but because they have received it from God and it now begins to change their lives and the lives of others. Parallels might be drawn with some of Jesus' teachings about seeds and trees that grow and bear fruit.

I have often used the illustration of the relation of the sun and the moon to explain what is going on here. The sun is the source of light and the moon has no light other than that which reflects off it from the sun. That reflected light can be substantial, if you recall how bright the full moon is in the middle of the night. But as bright as it is, the moon may not declare that it is the source of light or that it has its own light. It must accept its total dependence upon the sun for light. There are all sorts of things we might draw out of this illustration: The first would be that human beings have wonderful gifts and are capable of amazing creativity, but the source of these gifts is God. For them to declare that they are the center of the universe would be like the moon pretending that it can have light without the sun. Another thing we can draw from the illustration is that we are the light of the world when we declare that we personally are not, but that God is. This comment is not playing games with words. Christians and Jews have a profound sense of worth and confidence growing out of the embrace of their creaturely role at the hands of God the Creator. To accept the limits of our life can be the source of humility;

to set aside pretensions to be gods relieves one of a great deal of nonsense and frantic activity.

Now back to the question: can Christians possess the light without it being affected by finitude and sin? Well, Christians are divided on this issue: some say yes, because they hold that the Bible, the church or doctrine are exceptions to the general rule of human corruptibility. Others say no, because they think our own experience and history teach us that even the most valuable components of our faith are subject to the same problems we face all the time. That was the quick answer. Here is just a bit more.

Groups like Roman Catholics and conservative Protestants argue that there are exceptions to the rule that in this world everything is subject to finitude and sin. Some will say that the Bible constitutes a book inspired by the Holy Spirit so that it is beyond error. Others will say that the church itself is the exception. When the church gathers in accordance with its proper procedures and issues rulings, those are infallible. And finally, some will say that church doctrine should also be considered exempt from the limitations of language and historical context, so that it is good for all time. I call these three answers three Mighty Fortresses established to overcome doubt and error: an infallible Bible, church, and doctrine. Each claims absolute certainty because it is exempt from the limitations human beings usually encounter.

The problem is that these attempts to avoid uncertainty only spawn doubt and uncertainty, as well as a great deal of anger. It simply is impossible to make the case that the Bible is without factual error, conflict of ideas, or does not give sanction to things we don't accept (e.g., six days of creation, subordination of women, monarchy, and slavery). And as the scandals of the Roman Catholic clergy make clear, it is difficult to argue that the church is without sin. The irony of these attempts to protect people from uncertainty and the erosion of faith is that great numbers have been driven out as refugees, still religious but alienated from their former churches.

Liberal and mainline Protestants have been willing to accept that the Bible, church, and doctrine suffer the problems of finitude and sin. If there is any exception to this rule, it would be what is affirmed in the Nicene Creed regarding Jesus Christ, namely that he is like us in all respects but without sin. That is, he remained faithful to God and for this reason Christians refer to Jesus as the true Light. The best way to understand this view is with the concept of paradox. This is to suggest that God uses things of this world—even finite and sinful human beings like Moses and Paul—to impart light. Using Paul's own words, one can say that we have the treasure of God's light in earthen vessels. Therefore our understanding of the light and our proclamation of the light will be affected by our perspectives, our context, and all of our biases. People in this tradition affirm the Bible as the primary authority but do not claim it is, word for word, infallible. So for example, I think Paul got it right on Jesus Christ as the agent of reconciliation, but missed it on his view toward women and slavery. (If one takes the view that Paul did not write the passages which subordinate women or affirm slavery, one protects Paul but transfers the debate to how and why these passages made their way into Scripture.)

Liberal and mainline groups also look to creeds and teachings of the church for authoritative guidance, but they do not insist that they are absolute. As the world changes and as we seek to deal with new issues, there will always be the need for new ways to understand the light present in Christ. Lest this opens the door to everyone claiming their own interpretation, those in this tradition usually affirm a balance of the individual and the community, each correcting the other. For example, Luther balanced his right to define the gospel with appeals to Scripture, creeds, and major thinkers like Augustine.

After all this you are probably wondering when I am actually going to tell you what is the light. So here goes. The true light leads us to affirm one God who has created the world and declared it to be good. This God has made covenants with Israel and a new covenant with Jesus Christ for the sake of gathering all people into the Kingdom of God. The light shines in Jesus Christ as the true human who was faithful; it shines in Christ in his suffering and death for righteousness sake, and it shines in God's vindication of this forsaken one in his resurrection to be Lord. The light appears in grace that welcomes those who have betrayed God and one another. It appears in acts of justice that give life to those yearning to be free from oppression and violence. It appears in genuine community where brothers and sisters discover the freedom and peace of Christ. Jesus says that those who participate in such life are blessed. They are the light of the world.

10

Purpose

Which Purpose?

Purpose has been the subject of popular religious books in the past decade. What concerns me is that too often the word is used as a psychological category to motivate us to grow as human beings. What I find missing is a discussion of God's purpose. This is the over-riding concern for Jesus, and in its better moments, for the church.

There is a wonderful scene in the Gospels where Jesus takes Peter, James, and John up to the top of a mountain. There Jesus is transfigured by the power of the Spirit. There is also the expectation that Moses and Elijah will appear. Then they hear a voice declare that Jesus is God's beloved Son—a declaration reminiscent of the baptism of Jesus. In Matthew's version of this story, overflowing with affirmations about who Jesus is, the disciples propose that they build booths and stay there. But Jesus says: "Rise and have no fear." We could not have a more powerful statement about the purpose of religion. The disciples want to settle down and enjoy the security and glory of the mountain top, away from all of the conflicts and problems in the world. This is, of course, one way religion has been defined, namely, to escape the world for the security of a holy sanctuary. But Jesus will have none of it. To their need for security and confirmation, Jesus admonishes them to get up and have no fear.

This story is not unusual. Whenever Jesus is tempted to retreat or find sanctuary away from the world, he refuses. At one key turning point, "he sets his face toward Jerusalem." In another, after expressing his own fear about the future, he still prays that God's will be done. In the same manner he tells his disciples to choose for the Kingdom, not to try to serve two Masters, and that the last shall be first. The point is that purpose—whether we speak of a purpose for the disciples, Jesus, or the world—is continually defined by the coming of the Kingdom of God. The followers are expected to live in hope, but to avoid trying to determine the time. Their prayer of expectation places trust in the God who is faithful: "Thy kingdom come, thy will be done, on earth as it is in heaven."

Not Being Sidetracked

Given the centrality of hope in God's Kingdom, it is a great disappointment that so much attention has been devoted to thinking about the goal of history in terms of an apocalyptic vision. Let me first help you out: the Greek word *apocalyto* means to reveal what is hidden. Apocalypticism refers to theories about a final redemptive event, which may include the end of the world. In most cases it borrows aspects of other Middle Eastern religions that suggest that we are living in a crisis where good and evil are in absolute tension. The only solution is a final, cosmic battle, which will bring the world to an end. The faithful will be redeemed and the godless will be lost, or in current idiom, left behind. Added to all this is the attempt to predict the time for this final cataclysm.

The primary source for this kind of thinking in the New Testament is the Book of Revelation. It is now clear that this book comes from a period when Christians were persecuted by Rome and in that situation, the writer sees the world in apocalyptic categories: good vs. evil, divine intervention leading to a great and final battle, with the faithful gathered into heaven. At various times Christians have tried to revive the Book of Revelation, proposing that the end time is now. This happened in 2011 when a group set the date—three different times, no less—only to find that they had it wrong. There are parts of conservative Protestantism which rely heavily on these ideas, now called biblical prophecy. It has great appeal for those who perceive themselves as outsiders, rejected or persecuted by social forces. It produces some unusual alliances, as when conservative religious figures support the State of Israel because in their thinking the nation of Israel must exist before Christ will come again. A popular series of books depicts fictionalized stories of Christians preparing for the end, lest they be left behind.

The problem with this kind of speculation about cosmic battles is that it runs totally contrary to the basic message of both the Old and New Testaments. It has more in common with neighboring religious beliefs in the Middle East than with traditional Jewish views of God's saving power. In the Gospels Jesus clearly tells his disciples that they will not know the time when the Kingdom comes. Most important, he refuses to demonize his opponents or suggest that we prepare for an apocalyptic end time. The disciples are called to respond to the coming of the Kingdom, proclaim the good news and baptize in the name of Jesus. The purpose of the mission, therefore, is not to prepare for the end of the world but to be faithful members of the community and engage in the tasks of teaching, preaching, and acts of love and justice.

Apocalyptic speculation about the end of the world has given a bad name to any attempt to talk about the goal of history. The problem is that a future orientation is built into Jewish and Christian thinking. God is always a God of the promise; the people of the covenants are people who live with hope that God will redeem the time. The word we usually use for this way of thinking is *eschatology,* derived from another Greek word meaning end or goal. An eschatological element is essential to the teachings of Jesus: he announces that the Kingdom is at hand, that it is coming, and that we are to pray: "Thy Kingdom come, Thy will be done on earth as it is in heaven." In other words, a key to understanding Jesus is to see how God's purpose is at the center of the message.

Competing Purposes

What happens when God's purpose ceases to be the purpose for our lives? Well, either we make ourselves the purpose of life or we buy into some cultural goal. The cultural goals are all around us. While driving on the Pennsylvania turnpike I passed a truck with this sign on the side: "Delivering your future." I did not know my future consisted of more stuff. Look around you and you find a society dedicated to acquiring more and more stuff, finding identity and worth in the quality of things to increase security and comfort. I could also mention social and political goals that draw people into networks of loyalty. The twentieth century is a graveyard to causes demanding absolute trust and loyalty, leaving behind division and warfare.

There is also the option that we make ourselves the center of life. Popular religion in America has developed this to such an extent that it is, in my view, the greatest threat to Christian faith. In effect, it re-defines religion so that it is all about me and how God can help me reach my individual goals of worldly security, meaningful relations, and personal happiness. When this happens, the overriding question becomes: Does God love me? Now the conservative answer to this question is: "Yes, if . . ." If you believe what we say, attend and worship by our standards, and of course, follow our social and moral rules, then God loves you. God's grace is therefore channeled to the faithful, if they follow conservative beliefs regarding the Bible and morality. Rules against dancing, drinking, or smoking have been replaced by a narrow set of social and political views, which of course include the rejection of abortion and homosexuality. By contrast, the liberal answer has been: "Yes, of course." Horrified that conservative religion wants to restrict God's love, the liberal response has been to proclaim a gospel of unconditional love. This of course is quite relevant to a society that makes acceptance and worth dependent upon performance. There is indeed something liberating to discover that God's grace accepts us as we are, even in our broken state. What is missing in this message of acceptance is the call to participate in the revealing of the glory of God in Jesus Christ. Without that wider vision of what God is doing in the world, the message of God's transforming love is reduced to a blessing on the status quo or a technique for self-help. In effect, the good news becomes a postcard from God: "I love you; wish you were here."

The commitment to one's self takes on a broad social/political form in the current popularity of libertarianism. In the name of the freedom of the individual, we are allowed to construct a world where only my interests count or obligate me. This is usually presented in the name of freedom from big brother and inconvenient government intervention (e.g., standards for water, food, and health), or environmental restrictions. As noted earlier, Americans are hooked on freedom and they are easy prey for rhetoric suggesting that the government is unnecessarily meddling in our lives. The message appeals to those with financial means, since they have the resources to achieve their goals. If you have the money to pay for what you want, then public schools and universities, national parks and libraries are unnecessary. There is also no perceived need for a financial safety net or even broad access to health programs.

But the problem with restricting personal or social purpose to my interests is the break in the bonds of a common humanity. For example, the affirmation of home schooling as an individual right sounds great, except for the fact that it isolates the family from other people—especially those of different economic, religious, and racial characteristics. As one home-school mother boldly affirmed, she wanted to be the primary influence in the lives of her children. One wonders whether this is freedom or captivity for the children. What is too often forgotten in the debates about education is that the public schools were intended to prepare adults for life in a complex, pluralistic society as well as teach the 3-Rs. Another example of the break in common bonds arises in the assault on programs for people in need. As long as the views are framed in polite language, it is not apparent that in the shadows is a world of the survival of the fittest. If we are no longer bound together in a common humanity, who will care for those in need of special help?

Jesus transforms our limited views of purpose by pointing to the Kingdom of God. By gathering the lost and disgraced into a community of table fellowship, by insisting that we love God and neighbor, he elevates us out of our preoccupation with ourselves and our favorite group. Jesus sees people as persons loved by God. He does not use people. He does not expect them to be expendable means for a program whose goal they will not see. Instead he declares that the Kingdom is among us. Right now there is love and mercy, liberation from demonic powers, reconciliation of men and women, rich and poor. The light shines in the darkness of this world, revealing God and the knowledge of our true selves. By drawing them into this light, this Kingdom, he enables them to become new persons. At one point he speaks of this as losing one's old life. John's Gospel gives us the image of being born again. Paul will speak of the change as dying and rising to new life. Earlier I played with the image of the center of our lives: by ourselves we have allowed our lives to be decentered; in the Kingdom of God life is recentered—not in ourselves but in God. We are drawn outside of ourselves to participate in the glory of God, now revealed in the world. The goal of our lives, of family, work, even religion, can never be in us, lest we lose life. The purpose or goal of life must be taken up into God's goal revealed in Christ.

PART TWO

Reflections

11

Naming Jesus

IF YOU ASK A question, you expect an answer. But if you only have the answer, you have to ask: what is the question? I think it is important to read the New Testament with that perspective. The over-riding question is: Who is Jesus? This means that we need to see a naming process going on in the New Testament. It began as soon as the disciples and early followers met Jesus. There are many scenes in the gospels that seek to preserve the initial excitement and even bewilderment created by first encounters with Jesus. But it was complicated by the fact that they misunderstood Jesus and even resisted what he told them about the coming of the Kingdom and his role in it. For example, when Peter finally gets it right and declares that Jesus is the Christ or Messiah, he then denies that Jesus will suffer in his attempt to proclaim the Kingdom. While certain names for Jesus were present before the final days, the process of naming Jesus reached an entirely new stage after the resurrection. It was only then that they finally saw with clarity that Jesus was and is the agent of God's saving power. In this situation the search was on for the most accurate ways to name Jesus.

This helps us understand why there are so many names and images for Jesus. Some are very traditional, such as Messiah, Son of God, and teacher. Others are quite imaginative, such as Way, Vine, and Morningstar. Some are well known titles but used in new ways, such as Lord and Word. And some appear to have had frequent use during Jesus' life but recede from use over time. For example, the title teacher is used quite often in the gospels but then does not continue as a major title. I think the reason for this is that the teacher-student relation did not explain adequately their relation to Jesus. To be sure, some teachers inspire and change lives. But seldom does one speak of a teacher as a life-giver or Lord and Savior. What is also clear about the titles is that the meaning finally assigned to them is not always what the disciples expected—and what we would expect—but a meaning refined by who Jesus was in his life, death, and resurrection.

I am as concerned about *why* certain titles were needed as I am with the titles themselves. So instead of beginning with the titles, let us begin with the need. The early Christians found themselves brought back together, in spite of their disbelief and fear on Good Friday, by God's vindication of the crucified Jesus. In the ensuing weeks, they realized that Jesus was the agent of God's saving power in creating a community of new life. This community originates in what God has done in Jesus, i.e., his life, fidelity unto death, and resurrection. It is symbolized by their affirmation that Jesus is the center of their life and guides them in proclaiming salvation to all people.

Given this reality, the names for Jesus are going to have to express two things: First, that Jesus is the source of life binding the community together. In this sense the significance of Jesus can never be contained in what the modern world calls great ideas, whether we call it monotheism or the absolute value of love. Second, the names must make it clear that the new life originates in the saving power of God and reveals God's goal for history. In this sense Jesus himself as the carpenter's son from Nazareth can never be the center. This is consistent with Jesus' own words and actions, where he continually directs attention to what God is doing in him and in the world. These requirements for names indicate that some names simply do not have the breadth or depth to carry this heavy load.

I will concentrate on four names and two images. Two of the names—Christ and Son of God—have strong associations with the past and therefore emphasize the continuity of God's activity. The other two—Lord and Word—break new ground by using traditional names in new ways. They connect with the past but indicate a new situation, which also creates tensions and questions. The images are vine and branches and the Body of Christ.

Naming Jesus

Christ

The Hebrew word Messiah means anointed. It is translated into Greek as *kristos*, which gives us the English word Christ. Given the messianic expectations in the first century, naming Jesus as the Christ declares that the promise of a Messiah is fulfilled and that God is faithful. In Luke 4:16–22, the image of promise and fulfillment is invoked without even using the name Christ. Jesus enters a synagogue and reads from Isaiah 61:

> The Spirit of the Lord is upon me, because he has anointed me to preach good news to the poor.
>
> He has sent me to proclaim release to the captives and recovering of sight to the blind,
>
> To set at liberty those who are oppressed, to proclaim the acceptable year of the Lord.

When he finished reading Jesus says: "Today this scripture has been fulfilled in your hearing."

There are other ways in which the Gospels emphasize continuity and fulfillment. Matthew and Luke trace Jesus' lineage back to King David. Luke places Mary in the tradition of women who bear children as fulfillment of God's promises. In all of the accounts of Jesus' baptism, the descent of the Spirit is a virtual anointing, akin to the reference in Isaiah just quoted. Likewise, in each account the voice from heaven declares that this Jesus is God's chosen One, the beloved Son.

But the real question is what kind of Messiah will Jesus be? If Jesus accepts a role as the agent or messenger of redemption, it quickly becomes clear that he rejects the political and military connotations the title might have. This is the root of the sharp differences between the disciples and Jesus over the expectation of the Kingdom of God. As we noted earlier, James and John assume that if Jesus is the Christ, then they may ask for power in the Kingdom. But Jesus declares he came to serve and give his life as a ransom for many. The confrontation with Peter over his inevitable suffering makes the same point. All of the traditional titles (for example, Christ, Son of God, and Lord) go through a process of redefinition that is not completed until after the crucifixion and resurrection. This Messiah comes to proclaim God's rule and to give his life in service to God.

Part Two: Reflections

Son of God

The title Son of God does not mean what we usually think. It does not refer to a divine being, literally born of the deity. This would be quite difficult for Jewish monotheists of Jesus' time to comprehend. Several important references to Son or Son of God are helpful in understanding this title.

First, it appears in the story of Jesus' baptism, where Jesus is also anointed with the Spirit and a voice declares: "This is my beloved Son, with whom I am well pleased" (Matt 3:17). There is clearly no thought of a supernatural being in this reference, but instead a devout and faithful servant of God, chosen and anointed for a purpose. In this sense the title merges with Messiah. The title was often used for leaders or agents of God, or in some cases, it could be applied to Israel. Paul applies the title to believers when he speaks of them as sons and daughters of God.

Second, on three occasions Mark tells how persons possessed by demons know who Jesus is—a striking contrast to the crowds, which can only wonder in astonishment. In one case, the person calls Jesus the Holy One of God (Mark 1:23), but in the other two cases the persons identify Jesus as the Son of God (Mark 3 and 5). In these cases, Son of God appears to imply authority and power, which Jesus uses to cast out the unclean spirits. By doing this Jesus not only demonstrates that he is on God's side in the warfare with demonic power, but that he has power over demons.

Third, in the long version of the temptations of Jesus in Matthew and Luke, Satan begins two of the requests with the words, "If you are the Son of God . . ." These are the temptations involving turning stones to bread and forcing God to save him if he were to leap from the top of the temple. In this context, being the Son of God implies access to God's power. Jesus could use such power for personal gain or even force God to intervene to save him.

Fourth, when Jesus is crucified, Matthew describes the crowd as taunting Jesus in his suffering and rejection with these words: "If you are the Son of God, come down from the cross. . . . He saved others; he cannot save himself" (Matt 27:40–42). The language here is so parallel to the temptations by Satan that we need to connect the two stories. In both stories we are confronted with the title Son of God. Does it mean authority, power, and special status? If so, why is Jesus condemned, rejected, and left to die alone? Whatever happened to religion as the means for personal

Naming Jesus

gain and fortune? Matthew clearly wants us to see that Jesus is on the cross because he is God's anointed and nothing will cause him to turn from his fidelity to God. Thus Jesus will not come down from the cross precisely because he is the Son of God. In this one dramatic moment, the title is redefined in terms of service to the will of God. As a consequence, we have an answer to the repeatedly asked question: If Jesus is the Christ, why did he die?

If we stay close to these passages, then we can say that Son of God refers to one called and anointed by God and given authority and power to proclaim as well as demonstrate the coming of the Kingdom of God. What also becomes clear is that people are led to believe that Jesus is the Son of God by his person, his words, and his actions. He draws persons into a new community of grace and calls them to give their lives to the Kingdom of God.

Now you may be wondering how I could talk about Jesus as the Son of God without bringing up the virgin birth. First of all, it is not clear what Matthew and Luke intend by this reference in the angel's announcement to Mary, other than to indicate that the birth of Jesus will be according to God's plan, as was the case with wives of patriarchs in the Old Testament. Since they load the birth narratives with references to the past, it may simply be that they want to connect Jesus' birth to Isaiah's prophecy (Isa 7:10–17). But Isaiah's words are not a messianic prediction. Faced with invading armies, Isaiah declares to the King that by the time a young woman shall conceive and bear a son, Immanuel (i.e., God with us), God will save Israel from pending destruction. There is the further complication that, if taken literally, the virgin birth undercuts the attempt to link Jesus with King David, since the genealogy presented runs through Joseph. It is also striking that Mark, John, and Paul do not refer to the virgin birth to substantiate any claim regarding Jesus. We are thus struck by the surprising situation that the early church relied on the resurrection and the presence of saving power in Jesus as the basis for faith in him.

This conclusion stands in marked contrast to the way some modern Christians use the virgin birth, with references to the creeds, to prove the divinity of Christ. If the intent is to affirm that God was in Christ, it may be a helpful image. But as you can imagine, it sidetracks us into a complicated discussion in trying to prove a claim about Jesus. In this sense it detracts from faith: it reverses the logic of faith evident among the early Christians. One does not first try to prove that Jesus is divine and then move to faith in him. Rather, one must first come to know the saving power of God in Jesus and only then is it possible to use key titles which express faith in him. The Christian message is not that Jesus is a divine being who simply appears to look like a human being, but that he was a human being like us in all respects, who revealed God's saving power. The New Testament does indeed affirm that God was in Jesus Christ, that he is the messenger of the Kingdom, and the agent of salvation. It is for these reasons that the debate over the virgin birth is of historical interest but only indirectly related to faith in Jesus as Christ, Son of God, and Lord.

Lord

When Lord is used of human beings, it conveys a hierarchal structure with degrees of authority, power, status, and degrees of dependency. The title also has long usage in Jewish faith as a name for God. God is the Lord who rules and the Lord who is our shepherd and our light. The prophets warn of a Day of the Lord. So the title has very mixed uses: when applied to human beings it can have negative uses (e.g., domination) but applied to God it can hold positive meaning. Since it is the masculine form of sovereignty, its use has been heavily criticized when applied to God and even Jesus. So again we must ask, how and why is it applied to Jesus?

We must begin by recognizing that the affirmation Jesus is Lord is one of the oldest and most widespread confessions among Christians. While we find references to its use in the Gospels as a title of respect, its primary meaning is derived from the experience of Jesus as the risen Lord. This of course is a new situation for the early Christians, where new language needed to be formed. The basic affirmations are these: that upon his death, God raised Jesus, that he appeared to his disciples, and then ascended into heaven. In this exalted state he is Lord at the right hand of God and rules over all things.

To confess that Jesus is Lord, therefore, means several essential things for Christians: First, it means that Jesus, the crucified, is Lord. This moves beyond the title of messenger by centering authority and power in him. It also represents the fulfillment of his own words that the first shall be last and the last first. Second, this is the work of God, indeed, a new work as the covenant of Israel is extended to all people. The exaltation of Jesus as Lord and the bestowal of the Spirit are the signs of this new time of salvation. Third, to say Jesus is Lord is to affirm that God in Jesus rules over all things—the powers of this world as well as demonic powers and death itself. For this reason the claim that Jesus is Lord was rightly construed by the Romans as a challenge to the authority of Caesar. Indeed, the early Christians may well have made this claim of Jesus precisely to counter the claims by the Romans. To follow Jesus is to stand in conflict with all worldly claims to authority and allegiance. This point is unfortunately missed in current discussions where the title is rejected because it is a masculine title. The title has value not because it is male, but because it affirms that Jesus is Lord, not our government, nor money, nor even death.

Having established the fact that this title, when applied to Jesus, implies his exalted state, we must quickly add that it is the exaltation of the servant and crucified Jesus. This is one of the most striking aspects of Christian faith: it can never get past, go beyond, or forget that Jesus was crucified, that he died as one condemned and rejected. The risen Lord is always the crucified one, who stood among us in our suffering and experienced even our death. So the New Testament delights in portraying Jesus' redefinition of Lordship. We see it in his refusal of Satan's temptations to seek worldly power and authority. We see it in Paul's glorious hymn to the humility of Christ (Phil 2).

We have then a very unusual situation. To understand the new reality of the risen Christ and the new life through the power of the Spirit, two crucial steps have been taken. First, the title Lord has been stripped of any association with worldly power and domination over others, in favor of proclaiming Jesus' crucifixion and resurrection. Second, a title normally applied to God has been transferred to the risen Jesus. The point of the first step has already been stated. But what are we to make of the second step? Within the context of Judaism, it is one thing to name Jesus as teacher, prophet, even Messiah. But to assign the title Lord to him requires explanation.

My reading of the New Testament and writings of the first few centuries tells me this: The early Christians are so convinced that God has done a new thing that a new language is required to describe it. Not only is saving power revealed in the life of Jesus, but Jesus continues to be the agent of salvation in the time after the resurrection. This is the time of the New Covenant, which extends the rule of God to all people. In this time there are signs that even the powers of Satan and death are overthrown.

Part Two: Reflections

Therefore, since God continues to redeem the world through Jesus, it is permissible to speak of him as Lord. This Jesus, the teacher from Nazareth, the anointed servant who was crucified and who was raised, now rules on God's behalf until the end of time.

How can this be explained? All the New Testament can tell us is that God has exalted Jesus to sit at God's right hand. This is a wonderful image but it does not explain much or answer the questions we might have. Does this mean the end of monotheism? Absolutely not. What is the relation of Jesus the Lord to God? All we get is images. For example, there is the repeatedly expressed affirmation of God the Father, our Lord Jesus Christ, and the Holy Spirit. Implied in this is the affirmation that Jesus Christ, the risen Lord, represents God to us. The Gospel of John affirms the unity of the Son and Father as a way of explaining the relation of Jesus to God. But even this does not explain the relation of the risen Lord Jesus to God. Since there is little concern to answer our questions, we are forced to accept the fact that most of the time writers are willing to leave unresolved the relation of Jesus the Lord to God the Father. Perhaps this is the time to turn to the Fourth Gospel.

Word

The title Word is found in the Gospel of John, a writing usually dated toward the end of the first century. As noted already, in theme and language it is quite different from the other three Gospels and most scholars rely upon the earlier three to reconstruct the story of Jesus. Some have concluded that John reflects the perspective of Christians in a Hellenistic world, while others insist that it is quite Jewish in outlook. Its uniqueness lies in its bold interpretation of Jesus Christ as Lord and Savior, filled with dramatic imagery and powerful narratives. John's starting point is the reality of new life present in Jesus' life and as risen Lord. Given this starting point, John draws what for him is an inevitable conclusion: Jesus is the source of life and light because the Word dwells in him.

The term Word appears throughout the Old Testament as the agent of God's activity as well as the means by which God communicates with Israel. In Genesis the creation is by means of the Word: God speaks and things appear and they are good. Time and again the prophets declare the Word of the Lord. John assumes all these things but now adds the dramatic affirmation: this Word of life and light is embodied in the person of Jesus. In one stroke of the pen John sets Jesus apart, explains how he can be the source of life, and also describes Jesus relation to God.

It is amazing how John's affirmation of the Word in Jesus is both quite traditional and dramatically new. When we look at the Old Testament, God is not the deist God, who creates the world, starts it going, and watches from a distance. Everything happens by the power of the Word and Spirit of God. God is all over the place. If there is life, it is only because God gives it and conversely, when life ceases, it is because God took it away. God confronts, inspires, leads, and directs. God gets in minds and hearts, loves with passion, and longs for such love in response. From this perspective, to say that the Word of God is in or dwells in someone, is not really outside the limits of Old Testament thought. Remember that we are not talking about Jesus being a supernatural, divine being, ceasing to be human. We are, in effect, speaking of the complete union of person with God. Given this unity, it should not surprise us that John declares that the Son and Father are one—united in love and purpose.

And there is something dramatically new in this affirmation. As much as John or Paul see the Christian message in continuity with Israel, they also see something new happening in Jesus Christ. He is a new beginning, where the power of God creates on earth a new humanity in Christ. So for John, Jesus is the bread of life and living water. It is from this new life in Christ that Christians declare that a new spiritual life is present in the community of Christ, nurtured by Word and sacrament, and bound together by the love of Christ.

To name Jesus as the Word says something extremely important about both God and humanity. In the Hellenistic world of John, one of the dominant religious views was that gods exist, but they transcend finite existence. The gods represent true being, goodness, and beauty, whereas life on earth is fragile, subject to error and decay, and ugliness. As a consequence, one solution was to get out of this finite existence. If, as some suggested, the human soul took a wrong turn and has been trapped in a physical body, then we ought to seek ways to rise above such physical existence to a heavenly realm of pure spiritual existence. Two things stand out in this view: one is that our bodies are the problem; the other is that the true god would never come into this world of bodies. This brief journey into the ancient world helps us see what is unique about John's perspective. John affirms that God created the world, that it is good, and that God dwells among us in Word and Spirit. This is not slumming for God; rather it is what it means to be the God of creation: to be present in our lives.

At the same time the affirmation of the Incarnation says something important about human life. God has created it and redeemed it. Human beings are capable of being in relation to God. Even more, a human being may be filled with Word and Spirit and still be human. It is not the loss of our freedom or our humanity to love God, to give our lives to God, or to commit our wills to God's purpose. For centuries, Christians have made this point: Jesus does not lose his humanity in this relation with God. I think this offers an extremely powerful challenge to the current obsession with individual autonomy. For several generations we have lived with fears that relations with other people (friendship, romance, marriage, parenthood) threaten the identity and independence of the individual. We are not sure how close we can get to one another without losing something. My space becomes a special issue. The same concerns have been raised regarding God. Does not the Christian call to love and serve God mean the loss of my own identity and independence? If parents or spouse have a way of dominating, can you imagine how God could dominate my life? John's answer is that we are made for life with God and one another. Being in relation is not the loss of life but its fulfillment. Only in sharing life and love do we find our true identity and freedom. Perhaps this is the reason why John develops the Father-Son relation, a relation of purpose and love. What is interesting about this relation is that it is not exclusive. It actually becomes the great circle of love: the Father loves the Son and the Son loves the disciples; the disciples are to show forth the love of God to the world so that the whole world will love God.

The Body of Christ; Vine and Branches

These two images are extremely influential in the life of Christian communities. One is the Pauline metaphor of the Body of Christ, and the other is John's metaphor of the vine and branches. Both are organic images, that is, they describe relations between members of a living body. And both affirm the priority of Christ and the dependency of members on him. But there are also differences. Paul develops his image as a way to explain how diverse members of the community may be united even though they differ in gifts and roles. Just as a body has different parts, with different functions, so the church has a variety of members. Each has its purpose, but all are joined together in one body where Christ is the head. In other words, the unity of the church does not depend on uniformity but upon being joined to Christ and ruled by Christ.

John's image also emphasizes the unity of members, though it does not emphasize diversity of branches. But it is much stronger on the absolute dependence of members on Christ: just as branches must be connected to the vine, so believers must be connected to Christ. Being Christian, therefore, is not a solitary, go-it-alone existence, but being in a spiritual relation to the risen Christ and other members. John is not slow to draw out another aspect of the image of vine and branches: just as the branches can not produce any fruit unless they are connected, conversely, if they do not produce fruit they are cut off! The application of this image to the Christian life is clear: we are joined to Christ and one another to show forth the love of God, that all will know God and see the glory of God revealed in the world.

These two images say a great deal about who Jesus is and the relation of believers to him. Both reject the idea that Christianity is only a set of ideas or ethical values. Both emphasize that Christian existence is a new form of being, living in the spiritual power of Christ. So John can say it involves being born again; Paul can say that it involves a dying of the old self and rising to new life. To use the image I have employed, it means having one's life centered in God—in God's grace, love, purpose, and especially, in the community of those gathered around the table of Christ.

All of these names and metaphors give expression to the conviction that God has done something new in Jesus. It is amazing how they elevate Jesus, but in doing so always point to the faithful servant who was crucified. If they draw attention to Jesus, it is to reveal the God who redeems the world through him. He is the anointed one, the faithful Son, the exalted Lord, the one in whom the Word dwells, as well as the Lord of the community joined together in his name. He is God's way to us and our way to God, joining together heaven and earth.

12

Sin

Mission Control: We have a Problem

WHEN CHRISTIANS SPEAK OF Jesus Christ, the underlying assumption is that God has done something for us which we cannot do for ourselves. This says something about God, but it also says something about us. So let me begin with what it says about us.

Well, I guess it says that we can not save ourselves. However you want to name it, something has gone wrong. We find ourselves locked into a mindset, relations, and practices which do not create in us the ability to solve the problem. Some suggest we are stuck and I think that may be a very colloquial way of describing the problem.

I am quite aware of the fact that there are alternatives to admitting that something has gone wrong and that we cannot solve the problem. Let me be bold to suggest that there are basically two alternatives. One is denial. This is the general view that the problem is not really that bad, or does not even exist. It takes many forms. There is the rationalist view that reason is pure and untainted, capable of solving all problems. God would not ask us to do things if we could not do them—so goes one famous argument. The more popular form of this is simply the claim to innocence. This is rampant in America. No matter how many tragedies, oppressive systems, and acts of violence one finds in American history, the claim to innocence ignores the evidence in claiming that we had nothing to do with these things, nor that we benefited in any way from them. But denial is morally dishonest. As a nation it requires that we rewrite our history and invent the most naïve and pretentious self-image. On the individual level, denial does not work because it is impossible to hide our failings from others and even more so from ourselves.

The other alternative is just as scary. It is to believe that whatever is wrong is built into the nature of things. Little boys naturally beat up on one another and adults naturally abuse, oppress, and violate other people. It is the way of the world. Many people who speak this way are reluctant to admit that they are basically affirming that life is evil. But most of the time such pessimism takes the form of moral dualism: some things are evil and some things are good. This too often leads to the conclusion that we are the good and that the evil can be identified, isolated, and destroyed. This myth of good and evil reached epic proportions in the twentieth century, with great wars between opposing sides. The irony is that both sides usually claim to be good and demonize the other, making it legitimate to kill the other. Both Soviet Communism and Nazi Germany were driven by a messianic zeal, insisting each was the vanguard of good over evil. The goal is always to eliminate evil by destroying it. That is why twentieth-century warfare was so devastating and widespread.

It should not surprise us that this dualistic worldview involving conflicts between good and evil plays a role in the way most cultures think of themselves and their enemies. Military action requires that one first demonize the opponent before you kill them, thereby justifying the killing. The theme of good and evil in conflict therefore finds expression in the way we tell our history, as well as in our fiction, movies, and video games. While a long list of movies and video games are supposed to be for entertainment, they basically perpetuate the imagery of endless war between good and evil, with the bad guys dying. The more extreme American politics becomes, the more the imagery of good and evil creeps into the rhetoric and things becomes very divisive. Once one has demonized the other, it is amazing how all things become possible.

So this brings us back to the Christian alternative, which is the idea of sin. The primary meaning of this word is a break in trust—whether between ourselves and God or between people. To use my image of the center of our lives, instead of being centered in God, we are centered in ourselves. When this happens, we become dangerous because the people around us can no longer trust us or be at ease with us. In effect, sin is the attempt to use and control all things for our own interests—be it God or

Part Two: Reflections

people or the earth. This act of self-centeredness has been described in many ways: as rebellion, betrayal, self-love, and idolatry.

Once one starts thinking in these terms, one is faced with the question: How does one explain the reality of sin? This is hard to do, since sin defies a rational explanation. That is, it is hard to explain why people do dumb stuff, or even worse, unthinkable acts of hate and violence. For this reason we are tempted (pardon the use of the word) to think of people who do such things as crazy. Since *we* cannot imagine a legitimate reason for doing them, they must be caused by some non-rational sickness. Notice how this assumes we are wonderful thinking machines, which always do the right thing. But what if we are quite complex physical-spiritual creatures motivated by a wide range of things, including love, fear, and self-interest?

If you can imagine that, then you may be ready to consider Genesis 3. It is a quite sophisticated attempt to explain the origin of sin. But it is part of an ancient world where fanciful stories convey serious meaning. Rather than taking them as literal accounts of the origin of human life, think of them as symbolic stories which convey some truth about God and the world. This means you must suspend belief when it comes to some of the details, e.g., God walking in the garden, two humans in a garden where all their needs are met, or the attempt to hide from God. Instead, ask: What is it that the story tells us about the human condition? Here is my answer: God has created Adam and Eve, declared them to be good, placed them in the world to enjoy all things and one another. The one thing they may not do is to pretend to be gods (that is the meaning of the prohibition against eating from the tree of the knowledge of good and evil). So what happens? Along comes a serpent that tempts them to be like gods. The fruit is so appealing that they cannot resist it (it is a delight to the eyes and seems to be so good). Before the temptation they live in harmony with one another and with God. When the story says they are naked, we need to think of this as innocence and trust. Only in paradise can one be naked (physically and psychologically) without being embarrassed or afraid—after all, who can walk around naked in this world? But when they violate the trust by seeking the knowledge of God, all of the relations are changed. They are afraid of one another and try to protect themselves by putting on clothes. They also fear God and seek to hide. When God confronts them, Adam blames Eve and then lays the blame on God: "The woman that you gave me, she caused me to eat of the tree of the knowledge of good and evil." It only gets worse from that point. With the parents at war with one another, their sons quarrel and finally one kills the other. This is followed by the corruptibility of society in general and the idolatry of the Tower of Babel.

One can get sidetracked into the search for the Garden of Eden, Noah's ark or the Tower of Babel. But let's stay on course here and ask: What is the point? Let me propose something that may be a new idea for you. When Christians reflect on these stories and develop the idea of sin, there are two goals in mind, and both are positive. This may come as a surprise since the idea of sin is so associated with accusations, guilt, and feeling bad. So what are these two things? One is honesty. If one is not honest about the human condition, then things only get worse because of denials and cover-ups. The other is the idea that even though something has gone wrong, it does not have to be this way. Life is redeemable! It was created good and it still is even though corrupted by self-centeredness. New life can still appear. Remember that in the dualism of ideological warfare, the problem is that some things and people are evil and the only thing we can do with them is destroy them. The Christian story, by contrast, is a story of fall from paradise and redemption. Compared to the two options mentioned above, denial and dualism, the Christian view is both realistic and hopeful.

Augustine and the Traditional View

The writer best known for developing the Christian view of sin is, of course, St. Augustine (d. 430). Augustine spent years struggling with the problem of evil—on a cosmic scale as well as at the level of his own uncontrollable passions. It was tempting to adopt the view of cosmic dualism (at least two gods, one good and one evil) as an explanation. One has to admit that this view is very attractive because of its simplicity. Evil is real and it comes from an evil force acting on the world. But Augustine became attracted to the biblical categories of One God, a good creation, and a Fall from paradise to sin. This allowed him to affirm the goodness of all things yet also admit that something was wrong. His final acceptance of the Christian vision was the explanation that moral evil was not in fact an actual substance, but the corruption of the good. Armed with this constellation of ideas, he embraced Christian faith and broke with cosmic dualism.

Using the Bible and traditions handed down to him, Augustine affirmed that sin comes into the world as an act of self-centeredness, or self-love (which of course he knew a great deal about, having lived a libertine life). What distinguishes Augustine's view, however, is the insistence that acts of selfishness have consequences. They create a mindset in persons, reinforced by habits and practices. Since we are primarily creatures of love, the human heart, mind, and will become controlled by what we love, fear, and hate. But the consequences don't just stop there. What happens to the individual is writ large in the society, infecting the social structures, cultural norms, practices, and goals. All these things are passed on to our children, so that they too cannot remember a time when the world did not reflect a world turned in upon itself.

For all his penetrating analysis of the human heart and sin as an act of will leading to life curved in upon itself, Augustine added some ideas that have had devastating consequences in Western Christianity.

- For one thing, he concluded that sin was passed on from generation to generation by the act of procreation, thereby linking sin with our physical life and especially sex. Viewed in this way, all sorts of negative ideas have been associated with sex and some traditions have used this to defend celibacy. Augustine himself was a dominant figure, who approached the whole matter of sexuality as an either/or. If he was going to become Christian, then it meant a complete exclusion of sex and marriage from his life.

- At another level, the linking of sin and procreation gave sin a material status—a kind of moral genetic coding. This would imply that newborn infants carry within themselves the sin of the race and are subject to punishment. Played out in the life of the church, baptism came to be understood as the cleansing of the inherited sin. A side issue has always been what happens to dying infants who have not been baptized. One solution is emergency baptism, which any Christian may do, whether it be by priest, nurse, or doctor. So great is the fear of dying in an unforgiven state that such acts become a source of great comfort to parents. I have even had Protestant ministers tell me that they have baptized dying infants—and even ones already dead—as a demonstration of the love of God for the child and the parents.

- If sin is passed through procreation, a new rationale arose for the Virgin Birth, i.e., Jesus must be spared this transmission of sin. The claim of a virgin birth removes a male parent, but still leaves Mary as a human mother. In the nineteenth century the Roman Catholic Church adopted what had been argued for some time, namely, that Mary was born of her parents without sin in the doctrine of the Immaculate Conception. So this doctrine does not refer to Jesus but to Mary. The logic is that now Jesus is exempt from the transmission of sin from Joseph and Mary. Now you know why parishes all over the country are named Immaculate Conception!

Augustine Revised

The phrase used most often to describe the transmission of sin for Augustine is original sin. Most people cringe at the sound of the words, assuming it is like a curse which condemns us. The idea has been roundly criticized in liberal culture as being negative and pessimistic. And when you throw in the problems relating to the transmission of sin just mentioned, it takes a lot of effort to explain. But what if one extracts the original idea (pardon the pun) from all this business of physical transmission? Actually Augustine never blamed his body for his excessive abuse of wine and sexual desire. Rather, he blamed his selfishness and uncontrollable will. Abuse of food and sex are spiritual faults, whereby we develop habits and ultimately addictions, based on our acts of will. Indeed, Augustine saw the irony here, namely, that our compulsive behavior starts out as an act justified by mind and heart to create happiness. But the fact that we become victims of our own bad choices does not remove our responsibility for the end result.

The point is that we can provide a completely adequate explanation for Augustine's experience without resorting to the sexual transmission of sin. Using psychological, social, and historical categories we can explain how self-centeredness, love and hate, compulsive habits, and practices, are transmitted from one generation to another. The idea of original sin, reformulated and separated from sexual transmission, can therefore become a powerful category for understanding the relation between generations and the way sin has consequences that dominate and oppress. For example, one cannot read about the origin of World War II without confronting the idea that one cause lies in the horrendous terms of surrender imposed on the losers by the U.S., England, and their allies at the end of World War I. Coupled with the economic, political, and religious tensions in Germany and Austria, what plays out in Nazi Germany is hardly a surprise.

The reference to the world wars is not irrelevant to the revival and revision of Augustine's ideas. In its traditional form, the ideas of a *fall* and *original sin* do indeed appear magical and pessimistic. Liberal culture shunned these ideas and claimed instead innocence and optimism regarding the human condition. It assumed reason, education, and a natural good will would solve all problems. The crash came, however, with World War I, when Europe and America discovered the unspeakable violence unleashed by hearts and minds. Whatever naïve optimism and claims to innocence remained were swept away by World War II, the genocide against Jews and, in America, the admission of a long history of racial violence. These events forced many to return to the realism contained in the view of sin, only without the magical framework suggested by Augustine. There simply was no way to understand the tragedies of the time if the only categories we have are innocence and optimism regarding reason and the human will.

By the mid-twentieth century, therefore, a revised version of Augustine offered a realistic appraisal of the human condition. Instead of locating the Fall in a mythical paradise, the idea now pointed to the transition from unity to separation, from harmony to disharmony, which every person passes through. Since the process has been happening for thousands of years, it has had cumulative effects in creating an environment of selfishness and violence. Suddenly the language which had been deemed pessimistic was revived to create a new understanding of ourselves and the social forces at work among groups and nations: rebellion, alienation, oppression, greed, hatred, blindness, sickness, even bondage. How else would one explain the conflicts among people, be it family disputes or the larger conflicts of nations? In this new situation we have no difficulty saying that a child may come into the world innocent, but is born into a world already at war. In fact, we readily speak of the physical and psychological damage done to the unborn child by the parents. In other words, at birth we do indeed receive an inheritance of sorrows passed on by parents and society.

But lest this realism be seen as all negative, let me again remind you of the hopeful elements contained in this view: On the one hand it affirms that the creation is good; no matter how bad our description of the evils we face, the world was not created this way. In other words, the dualism of good and evil is ruled out. On the other hand, by insisting that the world is fallen, Christian realism points to the possibility of the world being redeemed. There is still a word of hope to be heard.

13

Good News

IN GREEK THE WORD *gospel* means good news. In what way is the story of Jesus good news? And for whom? Consider two testimonies by students in seminary. The first spoke in the morning chapel service and told a well-known story: he had fallen on hard times, suffered the pain of alcoholism and its resulting problems of failure and exclusion, but grace picked him up and brought him back to life. The message was straightforward: I did wrong, but Christ forgave me and restored my life. It's all about amazing grace. A very different story appeared in the life of another student. We were discussing a paper she had written, describing her personal journey leading to a call to ministry. In the section on her faith she affirmed that Jesus forgave all her sins. This is a standard way to affirm the importance of Jesus in one's life. I am not sure what prompted me to ask, but I thought I would move the discussion forward by asking: What sins did he forgive? (Let me note here that students do not have to answer questions if they are too personal.) What shocked both of us was that she could not think of any. So I asked her why Jesus was important to her. It took some time to get to the heart of the matter, but it went like this: she was the first member of her family to study beyond high school, grew up in a family culture which subordinated women, and felt thoroughly unworthy. She was ashamed of the poverty of her family, but especially suffered from the shame of being a woman, i.e., someone supposedly without worth. For her, Jesus was the one who affirmed that she was a human being, a child of God, valued and of worth. You can imagine that we both were

Good News

overwhelmed by this response. Jesus was indeed Lord and Savior, but for a very different reason than the one given by the chapel speaker. Yes, I asked that she rewrite her paper and she readily agreed. She finally had verbalized what saving power meant for her in words that described her experience. Note that for her to do this, she had to break out of the limitations of speaking only in terms of the images of sin, guilt, and forgiveness.

The contrast between these two spiritual journeys is striking. A colleague helped me understand the difference. When we do things against God, other people, or even ourselves, we may feel guilt and the need of forgiveness. However, those suffering from shame do not need to be forgiven—they inherited the shame—but need to be liberated. Now of course there are many cases where the two problems merge, as when we bring shame on ourselves by our own action. But before we complicate things, stay with the basic distinction. There are different forms of need and suffering. One solution does not fit all. Good news must take many forms. All we have to do is look around us to see how people we know suffer in different ways. In a single day you may send a card to someone facing death because of cancer, speak to a young person about finding meaning, read about violent conflict between opposing sides somewhere in the world, and wish that a friend would cut back on his drinking. Human needs take different forms when dealing with death, loss of hope, social conflict, or lack of self-control.

So what are these different forms of saving power? We have already named two: forgiveness and liberation. In the case of forgiveness, we have the act of acceptance in the face of disobedience and betrayal. At its heart is the unconditional love of God, which claims us in spite of what we have done. This experience of unmerited grace—which we have glimpses of in friendship and human love—stands behind so many interpretations of Jesus. In its simplest form it is the affirmation of wondrous love that gives back life when it seemed lost. At other times it has been described as God's way of covering or taking away the very thing that divides and has power to wound. You may have recollections from worship services where it was declared that Christ "takes away our sin." No one ever tells us where he takes them! I think the answer is that he takes them into his life and covers them with the love of God. And of course, the imagery of forgiveness often includes reference to how we are restored to a new relation with God by means of the life of Jesus. This has prompted Christians in every age to say that he gave his life for us. Finally, some have been

Part Two: Reflections

struck by the irony that Jesus the innocent one gives his life for the guilty. This has led them to say that he died in our place as well as for us. While a slightly different aspect is lifted up in all of these affirmations of forgiveness, they all share the conviction that forgiveness results from a grace revealed in Jesus.

In the case of liberation, we move in a different direction. Here the assumption is that we are subject to forces beyond our control. At first glance, this sounds strange and we brace ourselves fearing a discussion of the strange forces of science fiction. But we readily use words like addiction and social influences and pressures. Both the political Left and Right speak of the government as oppressive of individual rights—they just don't agree on which rights are being trampled. At times the rhetoric of either side reaches an apocalyptic level in charges that the government is evil and needs to be opposed. Or consider the way in which cultures and nations become caught up in ways of thinking that lead to destruction. For example, one of the saddest moments in twentieth-century history is the period before World War I. Everyone saw the war coming but no one could stop it! In retrospect, one comes away from reading about it convinced they had lost their minds. Christians name these experiences of loss of control as being in bondage to self-interest and/or the vices of anger, hate, greed, and fear. In other words, we need to be liberated.

The early Christians experienced a cluster of life-changing events involving loss of control and liberation: a man possessed by demons is freed, women excluded from the inner circle of authority and influence are suddenly given new status, a person living in shame is released and given worth, people living in the fear of death are empowered to live—in fact, one writer argues that we know Jesus was raised from the dead because Christians no longer fear death. All of these events share the sense that something has happened to people: they are released from what may be called bondage; they are given the freedom to live life anew. In some cases the loss is self-imposed. (This does not diminish the power which controls us, it only means that we have to take responsibility for it.) But in most cases they are forces beyond our control which hold us captive. Paul refers to them as religious and class divisions, sin and death, as well as the principalities and powers of this world. All of these, says Paul, have been overcome by the power of God in Christ, who sets us free to be sons and daughters of God, children of light.

Good News

There are no limits to the ways the theme of liberation plays out in Christian history, theology, preaching, hymns, and art. In the twentieth century the victory over totalitarian forces in World War II prompted renewed interest in the imagery of Christus Victor. When a new cathedral at Coventry was built, next to the bombed out shell of the old one, a statue of St. Michael, standing over Satan bound in chains, was added to the exterior wall. Since that period, liberation theology has become a worldwide phenomenon, allowing people to name their problems in terms of oppression by social, political, and economic forces. For them Christ has become the Liberator, who stands with them in their suffering and also gives to them the freedom to claim their full humanity. So we find the imagery of liberation used by the dispossessed in Latin America, Africa, and South East Asia, civil rights movements in the United States, women's movements all over the world, gay and lesbian movements, as well as any group which perceives itself excluded from the fullness of life. These images of liberation testify to the fact that saving power means the freedom to be human: to be free from arbitrary and oppressive limits and to grow to full humanity as members of a community of love and service. The images remind us that the gospel is more than a quiet word of forgiveness to the individual, but envisions all of life redeemed by the liberating power of God.

But forgiveness and liberation do not exhaust the ways saving power has been interpreted. A third group of interpreters affirm all that has been said, but wish to gather up all these things into a higher level of understanding. For them Jesus is more than an emergency rescue worker. He is the fulfillment of God's purpose for creation. Key to these interpretations is the emphasis on Jesus as the Word made flesh, who by virtue of the new spiritual reality present in him, ushers in a new creation.

As one might expect, this rich and powerful idea finds development in several ways. In one of the earliest, Christ is the renewal of the creation. Since the first Adam failed by his disobedience, Jesus is the Second Adam, who inaugurates the true humanity. Empowered by the risen Christ, humanity is liberated from sin and death, capable of being sons and daughters of God.

A second view sees Christ as a restoration of the original harmony that existed between God and the entire creation. Since sin has disrupted the beauty and harmony of all of these relations, God cannot allow the creation to languish in captivity to Satan. So Christ appears as the true

Adam, the faithful Son of God, who offers to God the trust and love needed to restore the creation to God's purpose and glorious beauty.

But there is more. Another branch of this family sees Christ as the last Adam, the completion of all of God's purposes for humanity. The entire creation has aimed at the new life that now appears in him, and the extension of that new humanity through the power of the Spirit in the community of Christ.

In these three examples the emphasis falls upon the fulfillment of the eternal purposes for the creation. They all are heavily weighted toward the new life—relying on the themes of incarnation of the Word and the bestowal of the Spirit at Pentecost. So, if one asks this family why God sent Jesus Christ into the world, the answer is God's faithfulness to God's own purpose. One fourth-century writer declares: "What was God in his goodness to do?" Another tells a parable of a man traveling with a chest of priceless jewels. When one falls out into the mud, what does the man do? He stoops down and retrieves it, restoring it to its original purpose. Such is the goodness and faithfulness of God.

Finally, I would commend to you another group of interpretations that find their inspiration in saving power as reconciliation. In one case, saving power offers the hope of reconciliation to groups divided by ideological warfare. Each side claims moral and spiritual superiority, as well as the freedom from all conventional rules, even to the point of reckless behavior. St. Paul speaks to this crisis at the church in Corinth by proposing that their claims to wisdom and power are parallel to the claims that judged Jesus to be a criminal. But God uses the weakness of Jesus on the cross to reveal the destructive nature of human claims. Reconciliation is possible only when we accept this judgment against our wisdom and power. Even more striking is his conclusion that we are reconciled in spite of our conflicting claims and are called to live without claims.

Another approach to reconciliation assumes that we cannot be reconciled with God unless we admit that we have constructed our own idols. What we claim to know about God has led us astray. Therefore God cannot be truly known unless we allow God to shatter the idols of this world. It is only when we are willing to turn to God in repentance that there is the possibility of true knowledge of ourselves and of God. In this sense, we are reconciled to God only through a crisis that destroys and gives life. If you want an example, consider the crisis created by the civil rights movement in America. Only by admitting what actually happened

Good News

in our national history and confessing to the hate and injustice still present can the door to freedom be opened for black and white people.

A dramatic formulation of reconciliation in our time proposes that we, not God, are the offended party. It is humanity that is outraged at the suffering and violence of human life. In this situation saving power takes the form of God suffering with and for us in the crucified Christ, so that we might be reconciled to God.

I suspect you are wondering when I am going to mention the view that Jesus suffered and died in our place to fulfill the demands of the law, usually called penal substitution. Christians from many churches have grown up with this view and it was the underlying theme of Mel Gibson's movie *The Passion of the Christ*. It draws upon the logic of the law court: sin has violated the law and forgiveness cannot occur until the demand for punishment is met. Hence the emphasis on blood, suffering, and death as payment for sins. This perspective has had a long and rocky road, coming under serious criticism. The two main problems are these: First, it presents God as an angry judge who cannot forgive or love without a payment in blood. This is quite contrary to the view of God presented in the New Testament. Yes, there are many references to the fact that Jesus died for us, even that we are saved by his blood. But those passages affirm something quite different from the legalistic claim of compensation for sin. They affirm that Jesus' life and death are signs of God's love. In fact, St. Paul sees the grace that makes us right with God as contrary to the working of the law. The second problem is the emphasis on death rather than life. All of the views mentioned above see Jesus' death as a sign of his fidelity and love to God. It is his life given to inaugurate the Rule of God on earth that restores the harmony of God and humanity—not blood per se. Jesus responds to the call to dedicate his life to God and in this act he constitutes the True Adam. Unfortunately, penal substitution has turned suffering and blood into the saving moment. Now I must add that many persons identify with this perspective, but in a quite modified form. When asked to define it, they affirm that Jesus died for us—something all Christians say—without emphasizing that God demanded a death as payment. (For example, consider the way we speak of the sacrifice of soldiers: they died for us not because we demanded their death as an end in itself, but because they defended people and a cause.) But the war of words on this one goes on, with many wanting to move away from the legal image, with its focus on blood and death, and others insisting that it is the only correct interpretation of the cross.

What's So Special About the Cross?

If I have succeeded in helping you see that saving power takes many forms, all of which speak to genuine issues of need in positive ways, the question still remains: In what way are they tied to the cross? At least one will say: "O.K., I get the idea but I don't need to be reminded constantly of Jesus dying on a cross." The question is a good one. In fact, numerous attempts have been made to translate the story of Jesus into a message of love and forgiveness, detached from the sorrows of Good Friday. Or we could translate the story of Jesus into individual and social therapeutic strategies, methods for conflict resolution, or general ethical advice. So why keep talking about the cross?

The simple answer is that what Christians want to say about God and Jesus is writ large in the events surrounding the crucifixion and resurrection. It is, in effect, the center stage where the conflict over the coming of the Reign of God reaches its highest point. Jesus and the cross are not merely accidents of history, of interest simply because he happened to die there. Consider three ways in which the cross is the message:

First, the cross is a judgment of God against the world. When I say this I am using the cross as a specific event in the life of Jesus and as a symbol for any event where people suffer and die. One is tempted to say that where *innocent* people suffer and die, but why restrict it? All suffering and death caused by the conflict of ill will, hatred, and inhumane treatment indicate that something is wrong. Whether the suffering is caused by people intent on violence or is the evil we do in the name of the good, such suffering reveals the alienation between opposing parties. To use biblical language, it exposes the idols and hypocrisy of this world. For example, in World War I, nine million people were killed. This monumental loss was so outrageous that it exposed the idols of militarism and imperialism which were so much a part of that war. It also shattered confidence in the moral and rational superiority of all the participants. But within twenty years the powerful nations were preparing for yet another war. Christians keep talking about the cross because a word of judgment is still needed.

It also needs to be said that the judgment represents God's opposition to the warfare of this world. God did not demand that Jesus or the innocent die, we did. It is precisely because God is opposed to the suffering of the innocent that God will not rest until the world is redeemed. Such is the message of the name for a church in Valencia, Spain. There, close to the cathedral, is the Church of the Blessed Virgin, the Holy Martyrs and the Abandoned Ones. What a name for a church. One cannot go into that church without being aware of the tensions present in a world where the innocent die. The day I walked in I had just heard of the killing of five children in Lancaster County, Pennsylvania by an angry man. Here was another set of martyrs and abandoned ones. This is the reason Christians keep talking about the cross. God is not satisfied with the world as it is. To the extent that we are, we perpetuate the suffering and the death of the innocent. God's judgment requires change, not compensation or vengeance. So, the cross is a word of judgment and a call to repentance.

Second, the cross is a sign of Jesus' will to embody and proclaim new life. By his gracious acceptance of sinners, his opposition to demonic powers, his teachings, and his fidelity to the will of God, Jesus is the agent of God for us. He will not turn back, flee or avoid the opposition, even in the face of death. He endures the anger and mistrust against him. In his own body he bears the violence of the world as a witness for God. He dies as the faithful and innocent Son of God, forsaken and rejected. In the early church this was understood in powerful ways. One striking interpretation of his condemnation is that he could not overcome death if he had not first experienced it. Another view declares that he descends into hell so that the Word of life may be proclaimed everywhere, for how else could he have released the captives? Think for a moment of my summary of the many ways saving power has been described in the preceding pages. Whether it is forgiveness, liberation, reconciliation, or the unfolding of God's glorious purpose for the creation, one and all of these occur through the agency of God in Jesus Christ. What Christians can never get over is that God redeems the world through the crucified; the risen Lord is always the one faithful even to the cross.

Third and finally, the cross is central to Christian identity and faith because it affirms that Jesus, the Christ and Lord, shared our common life. He came from lowly Nazareth, identified with ordinary people in their work and sorrow, and lived among the poor. As the creed declares, he was like us in all respects, except for sin. He was tempted but would not turn from God. St. Paul extols the humility of Christ as he endures suffering and death, asking the church at Philippi to have the same mind as was in Christ (Phil 2). He is rightly called the True Adam. His exalted status as the Word embodied in human form has never been the denial of his humanity but its true form. In sharing our life we see what it means to live in the will of God.

In our time this theme of God with us has become the major source of hope in the face of insurmountable suffering and the shadow of death. This is in contrast to several generations ago, where persons seeking consolation were commended to trust the providence of God, which ordains things according to the hidden plan of God. Now, by contrast, one readily hears the admonition that we who suffer or mourn should look to the cross, where Jesus suffered with us. Even more, just as Jesus was crucified, so God is crucified in the suffering and death of people. In many respects this interpretation of the cross by Protestants runs parallel to the traditional Catholic practice of identifying with Mary, the mother of the crucified. As the faithful suffer the loss of loved ones, they find hope in the fact that Mary also suffers the loss of her beloved son. Like her, we shall be comforted by the God who raised the crucified.

What all this means is that the cross functions for Christians in a variety of ways. It is the sign of judgment exposing the pretense and idolatry of the world; it is the demonstration that God is for us, offering new life; it is a reminder of God's presence with us. So to return to the question: No, the cross is not a rhetorical device to attract attention or an intervention to shock us. It exposes who we are and what God has done and is now doing in the world to create new life.

14

The Church as the Community of Christ

Churches in Crisis

IT IS TRUE. THE church is broken and we don't know how to fix it. Several decades of decline in members and dollars have left churches scrambling for new ways to reorganize and bounce back. They have tried nearly everything, from media strategies, high tech, changes in worship and music, and almost irresistible offers. What so many are unwilling to recognize is that the problem lies in the way the message has been re-packaged by American culture. As a consequence the message is subverted and loses its power. Let me describe two ways this happens:

Way back when the leaders of the American revolution settled the form of government, it was decided that there would be no state church. This was not, in spite of the rosy re-telling of our history, because they all loved toleration and religious freedom. The majority in each of the colonies favored state churches, but different ones. So since no one could have their church as the national state church, religion was dis-established. This meant that it was a personal choice of individuals: each person or family could decide how and why they would be religious—or in some cases, not religious at all. What arose out of this so-called settlement of church-state relations was the idea that the church is a voluntary association of like-minded people. Each local or regional church was established by the members according to the rules they chose. This also meant that those active in churches had to persuade people to attend, join, give, and serve. Now, this system began to fall apart in the great social and political revolutions since the 1960s. The problem was that members discovered that they were no longer like-minded! This was due to the fact that people wanted to make everything an essential (i.e., social-political issues and not just a core of theological affirmations). As a result, the church started dividing with no end in sight: over issues of war, women's rights, civil rights, environment, economics, and of course abortion and gay rights. The sticking point in all these contests is whether one can be in church with people who think and act in a different (read wrong) way. So the fact is that the church of agreement is dead and we don't know what to do about this other than separate from one another in a last gasp effort to find agreement. But that assumes no one (or not even the kids) will bring up any new issue which might be divisive. As long as churches assume agreement is the basis for unity, there will be endless fighting and splits. The fact is, we don't agree on very many things.

The second cause of trouble is that Jesus has become uncoupled from the church. In America, one can believe in God or Jesus without participating in church. To see what this does to the faith and practice of religion, just for a moment consider two components of the traditional view: first, Jesus intended to create on earth a community joined by faith, love and hope; second, as the community of Christ, the church fits into the larger purposes of God to redeem the world. Now, when you uncouple Jesus from the church, you lose both the mandate for community and the call to participate in God's larger purpose. In their place one ends up with the basic structure of American religious life: faith and practice are all about the individual and his/her interests and needs. Whether it is the assurance of God's love, problems to be solved, or the need for strategies for health, wealth, and happiness—in all of these cases religion has been defined in terms of me! Add to this the free-market nature of religion. Since it is only funded and supported by individual choice, religion must be sold by offering a bigger and better deal on human happiness.

It is an interesting question whether the individualism of American religion produces the individualism of economic-political theory and practice, or the other way around. In either case, the effect is the same. In religion people see themselves as individuals devising a relation to God and/or Jesus to meet needs. In economics they see themselves as individuals in a struggle of the survival of the fittest. The increase of libertarian views gives expression to the persistent theme of individualism in American society. It is striking that both the Left and the Right demonstrate libertarian tendencies. Such individualism, be it religious or economic, means that we owe no one anything and are free to live without compassion.

My view is that the only way to respond to those who want to hang on to the church of agreement or who defend individualism is to propose a different starting point. That is precisely what I think the Gospels do when they speak of Jesus and the community he creates. What is so striking about the Gospels is that they never refer to this community as something they created. The passive voice is dominant: God has done something to them and for them. In fact, God has done something in spite of their fear, misunderstanding, and resistance. They were called and claimed by God's announcement of the coming of the Kingdom. We will never understand the church unless we are clear on this point. There is new life and a new community present in Jesus; God has done something for us that we could not do for ourselves.

A simple way of naming this is to say that the early church was overwhelmed by grace and holiness. Both constitute God's intervention in our lives. Because of this we can only conclude that the leading character in the gospels is God in Jesus Christ. It is Jesus who takes the lead in announcing the Kingdom and embodying grace in acts of healing, justice, and table fellowship. By his acts and teachings Jesus invites people into a new relation with God and one another (consider the Sermon on the Mount as an expression of this). But God is not only gracious, God in Christ demonstrates new life. The root word for *holy* means one, heal, holy, and wholeness. When God calls a people—be it Israel or the new community of Jesus Christ—the new life becomes a reality. It is only because new life already exists in the community of Christ that there can be an expectation that the community will be and act in a new way. All of the things Christians are expected to do (love, kindness, forgiveness, joy, be at peace with one another) are possible because they are the things already present in their lives with Christ.

Once one takes this new starting point several consequences follow: frst, this means that the church as the community of Christ is a gift of God. It is not our creation, something we own or control, but a new life created and sustained by God in Christ and the Spirit.

Second, since it is a gift, we are invited to participate on God's terms. This is signified by the confession that Jesus is Lord: it is Jesus, the crucified one, who has been made Lord, who rules not by worldly standards of status and power but by God's will to unite all people. For example, consider a dinner party: when you accept an invitation you are obligated to honor the other guests invited, as well as the host's menu, seating arrangements, and plan for the evening. If this is unacceptable, you should not accept the invitation, or upon arriving, leave. But as a guest one accepts the host's plan. So with the church. In the church we are called to be together in what is called the peace of Christ. It is not based on our agreement, our preferences, likes or dislikes, but God's will that we should be together in a new way, namely, the way of love and holiness. Of course this is radically different from our expectations or anything we have experienced. For this reason the Gospel of John proposed that one must be born again—i.e., experience a spiritual rebirth. Paul coins his own language of dying to our old life and being raised to new life in Christ. Both Baptism and the Lord's Supper reflect this new orientation. Baptism has never been withheld from a person because of gender, race, class, physical or mental handicap, or any other worldly distinction. Baptism marks a person not by the world's standards but by grace and holiness. Likewise, the Lord's Supper is a gathering where there is neither male nor female, Jew nor Gentile, rich nor poor, slave nor free—and we might add, straight nor gay. In the Eucharist Christians experience a new equality born of a common grace.

Third, notice how the church defined as gift and the peace of Christ resists the two distortions of American religion. The one insists that the church is based on our agreement, the other insists that religion is a matter of the individual and the church is not necessary. Unless we make a break with these two cultural assumptions, we will not be able to envision a church open to the new life of Christ.

Fourth, if the gift of the church is the invitation to live in the peace of Christ, then the Christian life is defined by gratitude, joy, freedom, and sharing the love of Christ. Life in the community of Christ alternates between remembrance and hope. It is to engage in the worship of God remembering the grace poured out upon us and looking to the future with hope in the coming of the Kingdom. It is at this intersection of remembrance and hope that the church finds its mission: to tell the story of Jesus, to share Christ's love, and to join Christ in the service of others. Conversely, when the church is no longer a community that honestly remembers what God has done (but claims the credit for its life) or refuses to proclaim the good news and be with those who suffer for righteousness sake, then the church loses its claim to be the community of Christ.

Many Forms of Faithfulness

It is hardly a surprise to say that Christians have difficulty dealing with the variety of faith and practices among themselves regarding worship, witness, teaching, and relations to the world. The fact is that Christians differ. Two strategies used to deal with this don't work anymore, for good reasons. One is to assume we are right and everyone else is wrong. Sometimes this is tempered with tolerance, especially among Protestants friendly with one another. But this approach offers no rationale why we differ and no means to appreciate the differences. The second is to assume that there is a core of essentials that all Christian share. These usually include belief in one God, Jesus Christ as Lord, the sacraments, and acceptance of the Bible as the standard for faith and practice. Everything else, and especially those things which are so different, are judged to be non-essentials or secondary. We can tolerate them because they really don't count. The problem with this view is that when one looks closely at the way a Catholic, Lutheran, and Mennonite view the essentials, one finds that Christ is understood in quite different terms. Likewise, the three would be most unwilling to say that everything else is non-essential. In fact, in our day, the big church fights are over the so-called secondary issues. To put it in simple terms, everything in our day has become an essential.

I propose an alternative for understanding why Christians differ. It goes like this: When Christians talk about saving power in Jesus Christ, they use words like forgiveness, liberation, reconciliation, new life, new meaning, or participating in a new purpose for life. In other words, what Jesus does is described with very powerful images. But this brings the preacher or teacher to a crucial point: how is the saving power of Jesus shared or transmitted to us across space and time? We are not like the disciples, face to face with Jesus, but are separated by centuries and distance. Now, what I have found is that Christians answer this question in different ways. They have developed patterns of grace that have become trusted means or strategies for sharing the love of God. These are:

Part Two: Reflections

1. Participating in a sacramental community tied to the historic church.
2. Proclaiming the promise of grace and responding in trust of the heart.
3. Being reborn in the Spirit.
4. Engaging in acts of love and justice (or following and imitating Jesus).
5. Participating in a disciplined community gathered apart from the world.
6. Joining in solidarity with Jesus who stands with those who suffer.

While each of these is a pattern of grace for communicating the new life in Christ, they are not mutually exclusive. Step back for a moment and think about your congregation and tradition. You should be able to find all six present, though one or two will be dominant. I would also argue that if one becomes so dominant that it excludes the other five, then it diminishes its spiritual life and threatens the viability of its church. But traditions can give one of these priority, which brings me to the conclusion: individual traditions differ because they have been formed primarily by one (or two) of these patterns of grace. That means that the way they establish norms, read Scripture, worship, think about proclamation and service, and live with all sorts of daily/weekly practices—the way they do all these things will be shaped and colored by the dominant pattern. To return to our three Christians with their church buildings on separate corners of the town square: Catholics, Lutherans, and Mennonites do many of the same things but think how each does them in different ways.

What this approach suggests is that there is a positive reason why traditions differ. Each has been formed by a positive vision of grace. Moreover, they complement one another rather than compete or exclude one another. We do not have to denounce the other traditions because they are different; rather we can say they are different because they are shaped by a different way of sharing saving power. From this general conclusion I also draw an inference regarding the health or viability of churches. In this new age of sharing and mixing, a healthy church will be one that recognizes its dominant pattern of grace and seeks to give greater emphasis to the other patterns. Now actually this is exactly what is happening as we share music, liturgies, preaching, witness, service, and communal life. All I am saying is that we need to acknowledge this sharing as a good thing, a good gift from God rather than the work of the devil.

The Church as the Community of Christ

The church has its origin in the new life in Jesus Christ. This statement of origin marks the church as Christ's community. It is a new way of being in the world—which even the members continually fail to understand and violate by their disregard for the things that make for life. As the history of the church and our personal experience make clear, the church has never been sinless. Luther had a striking way of expressing this: Christians are sinners just like everyone else, who mourn the fact and look to God for forgiveness and growth in new life. What sets the church apart is precisely the reality of forgiveness and the turning toward the holiness of new life. As noted above, it is not constituted by agreement on anything but its origin in Christ. But instead of creating chaos, it gives the church the freedom to be a place where people who are different, opposites, and even enemies may be at peace.

Now if we stopped our discussion of the church with an enthusiastic discussion of its origin, what we say would be correct but incomplete. Some will be shocked at this, since most discussions do indeed stop with an extended discussion of its origin, often extended by discussing how it is One, Holy, Catholic, and Apostolic. My contention is that we must say more because the church is a community in time and space, a multiple-generational community which remembers its history and takes action to survive and be faithful. It lives with a complex set of relations to the world around it, mindful that it is set part from the world, that it relies on the world, and that it has a calling in the world. For these reasons we must expand a definition of the church:

- The church is a community whose identify and life are tied to its origin in Jesus Christ and the bestowal of the Spirit.
- The church is a community that has norms for its faith and practice.
- The church is a community that recognizes the authority of Jesus Christ and claims the authority given to it.
- The church is a community that affirms a goal of history.

Part Two: Reflections

- The church is a community that affirms patterns of grace to change individuals and society.
- The church is a community which embodies new life in structures and practices such as: worship, education, fellowship, care of members, stewardship, public witness, acts of love and justice, relations with fellow Christians, call and nurture of leaders, and a physical presence in this world.

Several comments are in order: First and most obvious, one must start out by affirming that the church is a community or one never gets there. Americans are so inclined to think of religion as "my personal relation to God or Jesus" that the sense of community is broken. This is reinforced by the tendency to describe Christian faith in terms of the transformation of the individual believer and then to add, by the way, that one is also a member of a community. Unless we break this cycle of individualism, we will never know the full meaning of the gospel.

The last five components speak for themselves. If you look at specific churches as they seek to survive and be faithful in this world, it becomes apparent why these components are added. They deal with the day-to-day faith and practice of the church. A quick glance at the hot topics which are contested in congregations or which divide traditions indicates that they relate to all six and not just the first component.

Finally, in our day many churches find it difficult to give attention to all six components. In the case of the sixth, many fail to give vigorous attention to all the things that make for viability. These imbalances lead to serious problems. For example, when churches ignore regular and clear discussions of norms and authority, they end up with a form of deferred spiritual maintenance. People forget what governs faith and practice. They are therefore vulnerable to all manner of excess when a problem arises, too easily influenced by social and political interests from outside the church. The debate about homosexuality bears this out. It is a very difficult and divisive issue, but one which should be addressed by strategies within the church. When it becomes a hot issue governed by cultural practices and manipulated by political interests, then the church falls prey to tactics of division and demonization. But if there has been no serious discussion about the Bible for twenty-five years, what shall members fall back upon when faced with hard questions?

The Church as the Community of Christ

When churches fail to affirm a goal of history governed by the Kingdom appearing in Jesus Christ, they too easily become enamored with the polarized and violent visions of the end of the world drawn from what is now called biblical prophecy. But these predictions did not come true in the first or nineteenth century, or in our time. If churches do not know what it means to pray "thy Kingdom come, thy will be done on earth as it is in heaven," then they will either run after apocalyptic visions or let the culture define their future.

When churches fail to see that patterns of grace have a purpose in addition to conveying the love of God to us, then the church becomes simply a gathering celebrating a private message of love. Baptism is more than naming a child but a way to change the world! Preaching is more than feeling good on Sunday morning but a call to participate in the transformation of the world. The church loses its sense of mission when it does not see the transforming power given to it in patterns of grace.

Finally, when churches select only several ways to embody the new life, they become cut off from the fullness of grace. One example is the creation of family chapels, which alternate between worship, fellowship, and care of members as a way of surviving in a changing world. Another is the vigorous claim that true doctrine and/or the practice of the sacraments is the only thing that counts. Even the liberal claim that nothing matters but acts of love and justice tends to isolate the faithful from the sources of renewal and a vision of the future, so vital for sustaining the church. Churches lose their vitality if they do not practice a wide range of ministries that sustain their life and draw them into a complex network of the church gathered and scattered in the world.

So this is the church. Perhaps the best way to describe it is that it is a group of people which gathers at least once a week to hear again the gospel and reflect on what it means to be Christian in this crazy and mixed up world.

15

Sacraments: The Bonds of Love

IF THIS SUBJECT WERE a movie, it would be very hard to watch because of the bad reviews. Few subjects have more bad images and misconceptions than the sacraments. From different perspectives, the sacraments are religious magic, completely unnecessary, or the means for churches to intimidate people. So where does one begin? Well, on this subject let's deal with the good and bad together.

The sacraments have a checkered past because they are tied to inclusion and exclusion. There is something good and bad about this, but unraveling the two will take some time. First, inclusion. For most Americans, the sacraments are signs of inclusion, if for no other reason than that not receiving the sacraments implies exclusion. But here we have to ask: Included into what? Usually the answer is salvation—however that is defined. For many, salvation means eternal life. Therefore it is imperative to be baptized and/or receive communion.

What bothers me about this is the way it is formulated. Instead of keeping the Kingdom of God front and center, with the call to discipleship to participate in the unfolding glory of God in this world, Christianity has been redefined as a means for me to go to heaven rather than hell. In effect, it turns the gospel upside down. It makes Christian faith all about me: How can I get saved? You will recall that Jesus asked us to lose our lives for the Kingdom of God. Jesus is not selling tickets to heaven. Another way of saying this is that Christianity is not a first-century mystery religion, with a Savior showing us how to escape this evil world to find eternal life in

Sacraments: The Bonds of Love

heaven. The early church was faced with competition from such religions and repeatedly rejected them. So there is truth in the idea that sacraments point to our inclusion into the community of Christ, but the sole purpose of the sacraments is not simply to get us out of this world to heaven.

Second, there is also an element of exclusion in the sacraments, but not the kind most people have in mind. Those who have never been a part of the church in any way have not experienced the community of Christ or had the opportunity to celebrate the dawning of God's Kingdom in this world. One could say the same of someone who has never been in love, heard great music, or missed a wonderful family gathering. I think God intends us for life together in love and in communities of love and justice. So those who have never known these things have missed something absolutely important. But are they forever excluded from the love of God? I leave that up to God. The sacraments ought to be positive affirmations of life in the community of Christ, not fences or symbols of exclusion of God's love (or tickets to heaven). The sacraments are not the means to scare, intimidate, or threaten people. Does it bother me if God could love someone who is not part of the community of Christ? Absolutely not. How can I restrict God's love when I am in the community of Christ only because of that love? It is not for me to determine the final outcome of God's judgment of all people.

Upon hearing this view, many will ask: So, if I stand a chance of being loved by God even if I don't participate in the community of Christ, why bother with the Christian life? Actually, St. Paul had a question like this: if God forgives sins why not sin all the more so there can be all the more grace? His answer was rather blunt, especially if rephrased in everyday language: "Don't mess with God." His point is: if all you are trying to do is get the best deal for yourself, then you are playing games with God. I would agree and add: to ask the question implies that you really have not understood the meaning of discipleship. It is not about us but loving God and neighbor. If life together in a community of love and justice seems an inconvenience or infringement on your plans and/or freedom, then you have not a clue regarding the Christian life.

So if I have succeeded in making a clearing in the wilderness of misunderstandings, let me discuss the sacraments from the standpoint of Promise and Participation. As a Protestant, I will be talking about baptism and the Lord's Supper (or Eucharist, which means Thanksgiving). But I think the Roman Catholic tradition has made a very good point in affirming that we receive the grace of God in many ways. As a result, they add five other sacraments as signs of the way life is nurtured by God's grace: confirmation, penance, marriage, holy orders, and the last rites.

Sacraments as Promise

In Jewish and Christian traditions, God's promises are tied to specific things. In the case of baptism, it is the washing of water. This of course carries rich associations: John the Baptist preached a message of repentance and baptism by water; even Jesus was baptized by John. Then there are the waters from which God creates dry land and all living things. Water also sustains life. Even the Exodus from Egypt involved passing through the waters of the Red Sea. In the Eucharist the sign consists of bread and wine, broken and poured out as a remembrance that new life comes in and through the life, death, and resurrection of Jesus. Much of Christian art, hymns, and preaching focuses on the blood and death of Jesus as if these were, in and of themselves, the means of salvation. It would be more accurate to emphasize the faithfulness of Jesus, who is willing to give his life for the sake of the Kingdom. The key is that the sign points to Jesus: there is no getting around or beyond Jesus as the promise of God.

But what is the meaning of these signs? In Baptism the promise is incorporation into the community of Christ. One is marked by God, claimed and named forever as a member of Christ. For this reason baptism can only be received once. It is an amazingly egalitarian sign or promise: baptism has never been withheld because of race, age, gender, physical or mental handicap, class, or national origin. Its validity depends entirely on the promise of God—not the reputation or power of the minister/priest or the authority of the church. Thus it can never be revoked: one's life is marked as a member of Christ and blessed with God's gifts. All of these powerful things can be said about the baptized without implying that God only loves those baptized. What baptism does is name a person as a member of the community of Christ on earth. Since God seeks to redeem the world by means of such a community, this does make a difference.

In the case of the Eucharist, the sign represents the promise of Christ to be present in our midst as the agent of new life. When the community remembers the story of Jesus and celebrates his presence, it rejoices in the gifts of forgiveness and reconciliation, freedom from the powers of evil,

Sacraments: The Bonds of Love

courage in the face of death, the goodness of the creation, and the peace of Christ. The key here is that Christ can only be present as the Lord who gives new life and sets before the church a new future.

Since I am placing the emphasis on Christ's presence, let me acknowledge that Christians have engaged in long and extended debates over just how Christ is present in the Eucharist. The answers range from affirming a miraculous transformation of the break and wine, a spiritual presence tied to this gathering, to the human remembrance of him. At this point it would not be helpful to delve into the nuances of the competing views. You will not believe the number of pages written about what the term *real* presence means. What I take from these discussions is the overwhelming agreement among most Christians that the celebration of this common meal includes the promise of Christ's presence. For our purposes, let us simply remember that we use the word *real* to mean actual in contrast to imagined, genuine in contrast to imitation, and true in contrast to false. One might even borrow an idea from Spanish, where real means royal. The point is that the Christian life involves a living relation with the risen Christ. He promised that when two or three are gathered in his name he would be present. In the Eucharist the community of Christ gathers to remember and to celebrate his presence, which also means to claim the gifts of new life that he gives. Christ the King is really present and his gifts are real.

Sacraments as Participation

What makes the sacraments essential for Christian life and worship is the promise of God. With these promises the sacraments become the means to transform the world by the participation of the community. Thinking about church and sacraments goes wrong when we take them out of the context of God's unfolding purpose to transform the world. Indeed, baptism and Eucharist connect the individual to Christ and offer Christ's gifts. But this transformation of a person is a part of the larger story. Remember that Christ commissioned his disciples to go into the world to make disciples by baptism and teaching. Thus the promise is tied to trust of the heart and participation in the community of Christ as we celebrate the coming of the Kingdom.

Part Two: Reflections

Martin Luther was correct in linking the new identity of baptism with vocation. He proposed that we think of every Christian as someone called to a priesthood of believers, to love and serve God and neighbor. This vocational and transformational character of baptism is lost when the celebration is reduced to the naming of the child, or even defined solely as the assurance of a place in heaven. All of this jumped out at me at one service where a child was baptized. Reading from the *Book of Worship*, the minister asked the parents the standard questions, one of which is: Do you renounce the evils of this world. The parents said: "Yes." I was tempted to interrupt and ask: Which ones? What an amazing discussion it would be for parents and congregation to answer that question. After all, baptism is also a congregational act, whereby the members promise to nurture and care for the child as it grows to maturity. If this seems a stretch, then it only indicates how far we have digressed from the true meaning of baptism. This initiating act has everything to do with Christian identity and practice in the world. No wonder Luther, upon being tempted at his desk, threw his ink well at the devil and declared: "I am baptized." Baptism defines us and calls us to live as free and committed disciples, as agents of reconciliation in a broken world.

In the celebration of the Eucharist, we come on a regular basis (hopefully) to pour out our hearts and be renewed, to enjoy the community of brothers and sisters in Christ, and to receive again the gifts of Christ. Eucharist comes from a word meaning to give thanks. Unfortunately, in most liturgies for the Lord's Supper, this note of joyful celebration has been confined to a prayer at the end. Following the tradition from Augustine to the Reformers, the service has been structured around the forgiveness of sins, with ample attention given to sin, guilt, and the death of Jesus on the cross. This creates serious problems.

One is that while forgiveness of sins is a major theme in the proclamation of saving power, it is not the only one. Just as important are the themes of liberation from shame and oppression, reconciliation of divided people, the restoration of the true knowledge of God, the overflowing love of God that creates a community on earth, the restoration of the creation, and the unfolding of the glory of God. By having the liturgy focus continually on only one theme, the full gospel is not heard.

Second, and closely related, the theme of sin, guilt, and blood sacrifice generates a mood that is best described as somber, but more likely as depressing. It is difficult to move mentally or emotionally from the sorrowful images of sin, guilt, and death to forgiveness, freedom, and joy. The solution here is not removing all reference to our sin. Rather it is to rethink the liturgy in terms of the fullness of saving power. There are other forms of grace besides the grace of forgiveness directed toward personal guilt. Or, to put it in another way, we have turned the Lord's Supper in a sacrament of penance, centering primarily on Good Friday. We need a liturgy that allows us to move from Good Friday to Easter and Pentecost.

Third, as already noted, the focus on forgiveness of sins recasts the Eucharist in terms of individual needs and expectations. Of course that is part of the gospel. But it is not all of the gospel. When we focus only on it, we reinforce the individualism in American religion.

What would have to happen to create a Eucharistic celebration that in theme went beyond forgiveness of individual sins and in tone went beyond sorrow? In working with pastors I have proposed two things: first, that we identify other major themes in our understanding of saving power, such as reconciliation, liberation, hope, or life together in community. One could also use the themes of the great festivals of the church. For example, Advent hope, the Word made flesh at Christmas, the light of Epiphany, or the gifts of the Spirit at Pentecost. There are also seasons of the year and stages on life's way. Why would one want to use the same liturgy at a wedding, or a youth retreat, or at a planning workshop for church leaders? Second, instead of adding the Eucharist liturgy on to the regular service, which makes it a second service tacked on, why not recast the entire service so that from beginning to end there is one theme and the Eucharist liturgy is integrated into the entire service? With the assistance of pastors and organist, we did this at the congregation I attend. What surprised me was how quickly the congregation realized what was happening. In a service celebrating Christ the Light of the World on Epiphany Sunday, we read Scripture, remembered Jesus as the Light, confessed our comfort with darkness, heard the story interpreted in preaching, with hymns and anthems celebrating this theme. When we got to sharing bread and wine, it was indeed a celebration of Jesus the Light in our midst as a congregation—not lonely individuals. The entire worship became Eucharistic and the Eucharist was brought into our lives in a new way.

This proposal is not merely dabbling in liturgical revisions. It is a step toward participation in the new life that Christ brings, allowing our lives, so varied and changing, to be transformed by the fullness of the gospel. When the Eucharist becomes only a requirement four times a year, or is turned into a sacrament of penance (i.e., confession of sin and forgiveness), it constricts our understanding of the Christian life. By contrast Christ calls us to participate in the work of making peace and seeking justice, of celebrating our unity, and witnessing to the joy and freedom of the new life. This is the work of the Eucharist: to gather together again and again in the presence of Christ to hear what it means to be the people of God.

But What About Our Questions?

I always have a sense that when I conclude one of my pieces, you are probably ready to say: "That sounds good but you have not answered my questions." Let me guess what they are. One is probably a lingering sense that the sacraments are magical/mechanical transactions, the religious equivalent of a flu shot. Like the flu shot, all you have to do is show up, fill out the form, and pay the money. I would hope what I have said makes it clear that there is nothing magical or mechanical about the sacraments. They don't work in spite of our lack of interest or trust; the deal is not sealed by any amount of money. They are invitations to receive the presence of Christ and his gifts in the community that celebrates what God is doing in the world.

But if that is the case, why baptize infants, who cannot respond to the promise or participate in the community? As you know, a significant number of Protestant groups insist on restricting baptism to believers who are ready to participate. If one puts the emphasis on participation, then one moves toward this position known as Believers' Baptism. But as I have indicated above, participation is not the only part of the sacraments. There is also the promise. Luther and Calvin did not agree with the Anabaptists because in baptism they wanted to keep the emphasis on the promise. In fact, the image of grace claiming and blessing a helpless child became for them a symbol of God's wondrous gift given before we do or know anything, even given in spite of our sin. It became the great symbol of grace against any claim that God has chosen us because of our good deeds or even our faith. For this reason I like to see the baptismal font located in a central place in the church where all can see it. We need to remember how we got into the church and what sustains us even in our worse moments.

Two other concerns may still be on your mind: After all is said and done, isn't each sacrament just symbolic? And if that is the case, do they really matter? If by *symbolic* you mean that the entire meaning is brought to the event by our understanding, the answer is: No. In each sacrament, we encounter Christ's presence and promise. We are led by the Spirit to trust God. Again we come back to the purpose of Christian faith: Is it just to help you be a better person on your journey through life, defined by your values and goals? Or is it participation in the new life Christ brings and in the unfolding glory of God in the world? I think the latter is a better understanding of our faith and for this reason, sacraments matter.

And of course there is always the question: How do we free the sacraments from the abuse associated with them? There is no way to stop some from using the sacraments as the means to bully and intimidate, as well as exclude others from the love of God. The best we can do is keep before us that the sacraments are all about God's promises and our participation in the community of Christ. There will always be lingering misunderstandings, magnified by fear and the need of people caring for the dying. For example, it is not surprising that parents ask that a dying infant be baptized. In such moments we need to do the gracious act and baptize in the name of the God who loves every newborn child. In less traumatic moments we can discuss whether it was necessary for the child, though it will probably be most necessary for the parents. We can learn at least two things from such events: One is the power of signs and words. We are more than thinking machines. We are spiritual-physical creatures who are nurtured by words spoken and physical acts. Baptism is a case in point. The other is that there is something extravagant about God's grace and we should not be ashamed at risking misunderstanding by being gracious.

16

The Living God

It is time to speak of the Christian view of God, expressed in the affirmation that God is Father, Son, and Holy Spirit. I don't know if the place to begin is to clear away the weeds (i.e., nonsense and misunderstandings) or begin with the positive statement (i.e., the beautiful flowers). If I begin by telling you what the Trinity is not, you may not hang around long enough to hear what it is. So breaking with my usual practice, I am going to jump in and start with the positive.

The basic Christian view of God is this: God is the One God, who unites within the divine life three ways of being, which come to be named Father, Son, and Holy Spirit. This affirms two things: first, that the living God is simultaneously the transcendent and ultimate source of all things *and* present in this world *and* the power which gives life to all things. Second, that the living God is self-revealing. Let me explain each.

One thing is clear: the Bible affirms that God does many things and is described in many ways. God is the creator who judges and redeems Israel, anoints Jesus, and bestows the Spirit. God is named the Almighty, the Lord God, the Holy One, the Father of our Lord Jesus, and our Father. Christians never doubted that there was only one God, but how does one say all of these things and still make that clear? Just as important, how does one name God to keep creation and the story of salvation before us? The confession of God: Father, Son, and Holy Spirit answers both questions. There is only one God and God's very name is an encoded message of the story of salvation.

The Living God

Second, the Trinitarian view affirms that God is self-revealing. It is a statement about how and why we can speak with confidence about God. Lest you think that this is making up problems where none exist, consider our everyday experience. When someone says something important—be it good or bad—how many times have you thought: "I wonder what he meant by that?" The fact is that words and acts are not self-explanatory.

Recall for a moment that revealing moment in *The Wizard of Oz*. When we finally see behind the curtain the mighty wizard turns out to be someone quite different than what we had been led to believe. But this is not the only problem. There is also the matter of how God—understood as transcendent and not like this world—can be intelligible to finite creatures in this world.

The Trinitarian framework speaks to both issues. The acts of God are not fleeting appearances but point to the nature of God. The Word and Spirit are from the Father. What is said in the prophets and in Jesus speaks of God because it comes from the Word of God. Therefore the Bible does more than report isolated acts of love, it claims that God *is* love. All this is possible because God is by nature self-revealing. It is God's very nature to be self-giving and self-revealing. The message is the real thing. If God is Father, Son, and Holy Spirit, then what has happened in Jesus is not a passing appearance.

This general idea has specific implications: the transcendent God can be known in and through things of this world by Word and Spirit. The flip side of this is that God cannot be the transcendent God without being the creative source of all things who is present and active in all things. The Word and Spirit present in Jesus—and I would also say present in the history of Israel—are trustworthy because they are truly God, of God's very nature. In this way the Trinity becomes a presupposition for our knowledge of God. God, who is not like the world of material things, is yet known in this world by humans who are not God. This can be because God is always the Revealer, the Revealed Word, and the Revealing Spirit. God can truly be known because what is known and the means of knowing are of God.

This then is what Trinity is all about. It never involved detached speculation about God's inner life. For the early church it was always a summary, and a presupposition for, the basic Christian claim that God was in Christ, redeeming the world. Trinity is about God, but it also becomes a doorway into understanding how God is present in Jesus Christ for our salvation and how Word and the Spirit are active in the world.

Of course, what I have said is stated in very broad terms. Such a framework develops in different ways. Let me present two traditions of Trinitarian thought which come down to us today. They are not mutually exclusive but share basic ideas from the New Testament, creeds, and liturgies. But they tend to have a different focus and produce different practices.

The Confessional Tradition

The first tradition does exactly what its name suggests: it confesses the story of salvation. God is the Creator of heaven and earth, the One and sovereign God, the Father of our Lord Jesus Christ, who was anointed by the Spirit, and is the bearer of the Word. Following Jesus' exaltation to be Lord at the right hand of God, God bestows the Holy Spirit—the Spirit of life and divine presence—upon the church at Pentecost so that the whole world will know the love of God. In the confessional tradition, the emphasis falls upon the Trinity as a summary of the story of salvation.

The confessional approach emerges quite early in Christian traditions. St. Paul repeatedly begins his letters with greetings in the name of God the Father of our Lord Jesus Christ, with later references to Son and Spirit. The great commission of the risen Christ in Matthew 28 contains the formula Father, Son, and Holy Spirit. I think it is important to ask how and why the early church began to name God with these titles of Father, Son, and Holy Spirit. My explanation is that the language used to explain the story of Jesus is transferred to God. Remember that the titles Father and Son were already used in the Gospels and Paul to explain the relation of God to Jesus, though without the explicit Trinitarian framework. The Spirit is the divine power and presence (recall Jesus being anointed with the Spirit at his baptism and the bestowal of the Spirit at Pentecost). Thus the language of Father, Son, and Spirit is already present in the early church as part of the story of the salvation accomplished in Jesus. What happens then is that the very language used to elevate Jesus as the agent of God is now transferred back to God. Just as Jesus is the Word/Son of the Father and anointed by the Spirit, so the Word/Son and Spirit are affirmed of God. In effect, the story of Jesus now becomes the story of God: the Father who sends the Son and bestows the Spirit.

What is new in this development? It is not new to describe God as Father, or as Word, or as Spirit. Word and Spirit are images used throughout the Old Testament, whether we are speaking of creation, prophetic judgment and hope, or redemption. What is new is: 1) to identify the Word with Jesus; 2) to use the images of Father-Son to name God; 3) to affirm the Spirit of Christ at Pentecost as the Spirit of God. The positive justification for these moves is obviously the centrality of God's revelation in Jesus Christ, raised to be Lord and Savior. Just as Jesus is elevated to significance in the story of salvation because he is the Son of God, so now the exalted Jesus is identified with the eternal Word.

Does this mean Jesus of Nazareth is God? It is clear that the New Testament affirms that the Word of God is revealed in the face of Jesus Christ—the crucified and exalted Lord. But at the same time there is great caution in suggesting that Jesus is God. It is one thing to say God is in Jesus but quite another to say Jesus is God. This is not quibbling over words. The New Testament prefers to speak of God's Word dwelling in Jesus or of God acting through Jesus. Notice that the affirmations are always qualified: the Spirit descends upon Jesus and the Word becomes flesh in Jesus, but it confuses matters to say Jesus is God. The creeds share this concern: the Word and Jesus are not totally interchangeable. The Word is the eternal Word before all time, Jesus is not. In the Nicene Creed it is clearly stated that whereas the eternal Word is begotten of the Father before all time, Jesus is begotten of the Word in time, born of Mary. The creeds make clear that the Word in Jesus does not mean the loss of Jesus' humanity.

The great strength of the confessional tradition is its dramatic telling of the story of Jesus Christ. But in doing this it presents us with a story that is loosely coupled, leaving many unanswered questions. Its intent is not to explain all of the relations or issues. Chief among these unanswered concerns is: What is the relation of the Word/Son to God the Father? Rephrased, what is the relation of the risen, exalted Lord Jesus to God? Paul says Jesus is raised to the right hand of God. But what does that mean? He also says that at the end of time Christ will gather all things together and present them to God the Father. But no explanation is given as to what this means. The confessional approach leaves these questions unanswered; its purpose is to confess the history of salvation.

Part Two: Reflections

It is not surprising that the confessional approach emphasizes the threefold character of God, namely, Father, Son, and Holy Spirit. The three titles are deeply rooted in the personal language of the story of salvation. Their use in preaching, hymns, art, sculpture, liturgy, and theology inspires elaborate discussions of how Father, Son, and Holy Spirit relate to one another. It is not uncommon to find hymns devoting a verse to each of the members of the Trinity—telling a story in three acts. Specific roles are assigned to each member, with Creation, Redemption, and Sanctification identified with the three personae. At times the differentiation between the three members is so personalized that each is treated as a center of consciousness: e. g., the Father sends the Son, the Son loves the Father, and the Spirit is the bond of love between Father and Son. For those who worry about strict monotheism, this obviously makes them nervous, since it begins to sound like a central committee within God.

Another development, since the three members are rather loosely defined, is to elevate the Father to primary status. If one visits cathedrals in Europe it will not be hard to find sculpture depicting the Trinity: God the Father is a central figure seated on a throne, the risen Christ is being crowned on one side, while the dove (Holy Spirit) is nearby. In some cases, Mary is also included in the scene, recognized for her role in the story of salvation. In contemporary America, the fluidity of the confessional view often results in the popular view that Trinity refers to God the Father, Jesus, and the Holy Spirit. This is a very confusing practice, since it does not reflect the confessions of the New Testament or the creeds.

The Nicene Tradition

A second way of thinking about the Trinity is the Nicene tradition. While the doctrine of the Trinity was approved at the Council of Nicea in 325, the Trinitarian theology existed before the fourth century. By the Nicene tradition I am referring to the distinctive approach affirmed by the Council of Nicea, as well as succeeding Councils in 375 and 451. While the Nicene Tradition gathers together the confessions from the story of salvation, it focuses attention on the relations of Father, Son, and Spirit within God. At issue is the question: In what way is God present in Jesus?

The Nicene tradition answers this question by declaring that the Word/Son is embodied in Jesus. What is distinctive is a new section inserted into the traditional creed. There it affirms that the Word/Son is begotten of the Father before all time and is truly God. If one does not get it the first time, it hammers the point with the added declarations: "God from God, light from light, true God from true God, begotten not made, of one Being with the Father." If there is any question that the Creed is speaking of the eternal Word/Son and not Jesus, note the next sentence: "By whom all things were made both in heaven and on earth." Here the Nicene Tradition offers the clearest statement about God: It is God's very nature to be Father, Son, and Holy Spirit, One God. The three members are equally God and are distinguished only by their relation to one another: the Father is unbegotten, the Son/Word is begotten of the Father before all time, and the Spirit proceeds from the Father and the Son. It is only after this perfect equality of the Word/Son with the Father has been established that the Creed then declares that the Word/Son "for us and for our salvation came down from heaven and was incarnate and was made man."

What prompted this extraordinary expansion of the Apostles' Creed? The answer lies in the two counter proposals advocated by some in the fourth century. In the one case, it was urged that we hold to the Hellenistic idea that God is totally transcendent and so pure in divinity that God could not possible enter into the world of change and suffering. To accommodate the story of Jesus to this idea, it was argued that the Word cannot be of the same substance as the Father, but is part of the creation. In other words, the true God was not in in Christ, reconciling the world to God. But this overturns the basic claim about Jesus Christ. In the second case, there was a willingness to admit that God can appear as Son and Spirit and all manner of other things, but that these appearances are not revelatory of the true nature of God. They are only temporary modes of being. But if this is the case, then we can never really be sure that anything truly reveals God. There is always a gap between the word or act and the hidden God.

Against both of these challenges, the advocates of the Nicene Creed insisted on the strongest possible language. By establishing the equality of the Father, Son, and Holy Spirit, the Nicene Tradition affirms the unity of the One God. But it is not a unity sealed off from this world. The Word of God can become incarnate in Jesus because the Word, begotten of the Father, is already in the world and the Spirit is already sustaining and giving life to all things.

Part Two: Reflections

If the confessional approach emphasizes the threefold character of God, the Nicene approach comes down heavily on the unity of God. God is one and within the oneness of God there are three ways of being. In this respect our understanding of God is greatly enriched. While we usually think of the three members in terms of their personal titles of Father, Son, and Holy Spirit, they can also be seen as affirming three essential components of the divine life. One is that God is ultimate, transcending all aspects of the finite creation. A second is that God is by nature relational, i.e., capable of personal expression as the Word. And finally, a third is an affirmation of immediacy or presence with life-giving power. Viewed in this light, Trinity is not only a summary of the story of Jesus, but serious reflection on what we take the word *God* to mean.

The emphasis on the unity of God finds further expression in the insistence that all activities of God involve all three members. Every act—creation, redemption, sanctification—is from the Father, revealing the Word/Son and by means of the power of the Spirit. Notice that in the quote from the Nicene Creed the world is created through the Word. The three members cannot be separated by function but participate together in all activities. From this perspective it is not appropriate to substitute the functional titles Creator, Redeemer, and Sanctifier for the three personal titles of the members.

Let me pause here to add a comment about masculine language, which has become a great debate in our time. The debate has extended to our liturgies, prayers, and the Trinitarian formula of Father, Son, and Holy Spirit. If you are not aware of the debate, give serious consideration to the implications of using words like Father and Son to describe God. No matter how many times we say God is not male, such language makes it difficult to change patterns of thought. So what shall we do about the Trinitarian formula? The titles Father and Son have served to emphasize the personal character of God, and to assure the full equality of the Word with God the Father. Note that the Nicene Creed uses the language of procreation to make this point. The Word is not a part of the creation, fabricated by God into some form, but begotten, not made. This is a highly symbolic use of the word begotten, since it does not involve a marriage of Father and Mother. It is employed only to assure that the Word/Son is of the same substance as God the Father.

But even after we add this important historical note, what shall we do with language that relies so heavily on masculine images? My personal preference would be to speak of God as Source, Word and Holy Spirit. Another option would be to paraphrase some of the rich lines from the New Testament without using masculine terms. For example, one might baptize in the name of "The God whose Word and Spirit empowered our Lord and Savior Jesus Christ." Since I am reluctant to identify the three members with functions, I prefer not to substitute "Creator, Redeemer, and Sanctifier" for the three members. But I would prefer to do that than use a current mix and match formula: Creator, Christ, and Holy Spirit. But these proposals will not satisfy everyone. The fact is that these are very tense and trying times for debates in churches. I am opposed to requiring the formula as a test of faith or banning the formula. What we need now is a time of conversation, prayer, study, and waiting for new and creative options to emerge. God is a mystery but the doctrine of the Trinity is not a mystery. We ought to be able to find an acceptable way to express the central affirmation about the presence of God in Christ and the Spirit in us, in the church and in the world.

To close, let us return to the basic question: Why is it crucial to speak of God as Father, Son, and Holy Spirit? This question is complicated by the fact that for many Protestants the doctrine of the Trinity is inoperative, especially those nurtured by free or low-church liturgical traditions. They simply don't know what it is or how it relates to the faith they proclaim. To be sure, the formula is often invoked at the beginning of a service—as if the formula makes things official—or used at baptisms. But the broad and rich theology of the Trinitarian view of God—in either the confessional or Nicene tradition—is too often lacking. This is most unfortunate because it impoverishes our understanding of God. Without the rich Trinitarian framework, it is too easy to reduce Jesus to a teacher of love or the one who helps us solve our problems. Likewise, the church is reduced to an association of like-minded persons because it is not conceived as a spiritual union with Christ. Missing is the affirmation that God is present in Jesus creating new life on earth. Absent is the affirmation of the church as the Body of Christ, empowered by the Spirit to be an agent of reconciliation and peace in this world. What is needed is not another dull sermon on the technical terms of the Nicene Creed, but the bold affirmation that God was in Christ, that the Word came down from heaven—as the creed declares—for us and for our salvation. The Trinitarian view is crucial because it tells us God is always the personal, living God revealed in Word and Spirit.

17

Conclusion

IT IS RECORDED IN the Acts of the Apostles that when the Apostle Peter finished a sermon, the listeners were so moved that they said: "What shall we do?" To this Peter replied in words parallel to Jesus' great command: Repent and believe. What would it mean for us to respond to a hearing of the good news with repentance and faith?

As you probably know, the root word for repentance means to turn around. It could mean return, though we should caution against jumping on the band wagon for a return to the good old days, which might simply involve old forms of the same problems we now face. Likewise, it could mean turn away, which has a definite anti-worldly tone. For now let us stay with the simplest meaning, namely, turn around or turn from our present commitments. I like to think of the question put to Peter as the revolutionary question, since both words (repent and revolve) mean a turning. Those of you familiar with political theory will know that one of Friedrich Engel's revolutionary tracts was given the title: *What Shall We Do?* But just remember, they got it from the Book of Acts.

While Peter's response calls us to believe, I have always preferred to use the word *trust*, since *believe* too easily moves in the direction of a list of ideas held firmly in our heads. In several easy steps we move from believe to beliefs to doctrine, and thereby turn Christian faith into an intellectual project where the one with the most beliefs wins. By contrast, *trust* is a far more dangerous word, since it refers to the commitments of the heart and the way we bind ourselves to people and things. When Jesus says no one can serve two masters, I think he is talking about trust as a form of life's commitment and goal. But even I must admit that trust can be confined to the secret recesses of the heart and never express itself. Jesus' insistence that we love one another cuts through all the qualifications about head and heart, internal and external. As noted repeatedly, true faith is active in love. To quote a contemporary wise man, when Harry Potter confesses that he may be tempted by evil thoughts, Professor Dumbledore counsels him by saying that genuine character is revealed not by what we think or feel but by what we do.

Let me join acts of repentance and trust into one by reviving an old word. *Piety* refers to the unity of faith and practice, ideas and actions. It has been a word somewhat abused in my lifetime, since my generation did not want to appear pious. That suggested a pretentious show of religion and we greatly feared personal practices which lacked social consequences. As a result we embraced the world, without realizing that the emphasis on doing needed to be nurtured by the discipline of spiritual practices. All this is said to make it clear that the introduction of the word *piety* is not meant to turn back to anti-worldly or private religiosity. Perhaps the current but somewhat overused word *lifestyle* comes close to piety, since it refers to both the way we live and the values/commitments which undergird the simple and complex practices which make up our lives. I also like the word *piety* because it easily combines repentance and faith as a form of commitment and set of practices. Roman Catholics will easily understand this, since repentance has been elevated into a sacrament and become a regular practice, not just a moment of remorse. We also need to combine repentance and faith because true faith can never exist unless we turn from our false trust and practices. So Luther stated in the very first thesis, nailed to the church door in Wittenburg, that when Jesus said we are to repent, he meant that it involved a life-long practice.

It may be helpful to contrast different forms of piety. One of the oldest is characteristic of Roman Catholic life in Europe. Consider for a moment the faithful gathering in cathedrals and churches, shrines and other sacred places, to remember the crucified Jesus and the suffering of the saints. In its central moment, the mass combines remembrance and re-enactment as the faithful approach with repentant and trusting hearts to receive the salvation offered by God in Jesus Christ. The Christian life is structured around this worship, on a daily and weekly basis, and throughout the church year. It is what I would call a piety of adoration:

faith and practice directed toward remembrance and adoration of Christ, Mary, and the saints.

The Protestant movement of the sixteenth century cultivated a different form of piety. It called believers to hear on a daily basis the promises of God and respond with trust of the heart. This celebration of grace freely given to sinners was so overwhelming that the dominant response was gratitude. But instead of turning such gratitude toward the religious orders called out of the world, Protestants spoke of a priesthood of all believers in the world, serving God and neighbor. In this sense the piety of gratitude was an embrace of the world, originating in a retelling of the story of Jesus. But the problem this form of piety has always faced is: How does one keep alive the joyful and vibrant sense of gratitude? Forgetfulness and the sorrows and failures of this life make it difficult to sustain. As you can imagine, a variety of tactics have been used to revive and sustain gratitude. The obvious one is to retell the story, again and again, in sermon, Bible study, hymns, and anthems. Just think of the first verse of "Amazing Grace" as a reminder to the congregation to repent and believe one more time! But other tactics tended toward writing it all down and getting people to give assent. Then there were scary tactics of setting rules, using guilt, or threatening punishment (exclusion). It took a while to discover that these strategies did not promote much gratitude. But I have to confess that the piety of gratitude has been the dominant one in my life and it has nurtured and sustained me through thick and thin.

Yet another form of piety is one which may speak to our times. It combines our interest in the world with our traditional preference for doing something that is good. I call it a piety of glory: it is living in the expectation that the glory of God is now being revealed in the world and we are called to participate in acts of love and justice. Such piety commends itself by turning our attention to the divine purpose revealed in Christ. For one thing, it brings to the foreground the affirmations of the Incarnation and bestowal of the Spirit. It also focuses attention on the present rather than the past. And by turning our attention to what God is doing in the world today, we are prompted to turn away from our preoccupation with what the world expects the future to be. This is both an expansion of our horizon and a liberation from the limits the world sets for what is possible. In a piety of glory, faith is permitted to envision a world where, as the hymn proclaims, Christ is changing everything.

Conclusion

The three forms of piety are not mutually exclusive. I cannot imagine the Christian life without incorporating elements of adoration, gratitude, and a vision of glory. But as noted, it may well be that a piety of glory has the ability to catch the imagination of people in new ways. We should not, however, quarrel over which is best but draw on all three to find appropriate forms of repentance and faith. Consider these options:

1. We must begin with the new reality that confronts us: the powers of the world have been broken and we are enabled to see the world in a new way. Note well that Jesus does not say that if you repent and believe, then things will change. Rather he first announces the Kingdom of God as a new reality and calls us to respond to that reality with repentance and trust. In other words, Jesus is not selling floor plans for us to build new houses on our own, but asking us to come and live in the new house God has constructed. That is what is so powerful about the presentation of Jesus in the gospels: he draws people into the new reality of a community. They want to be there, but must learn to trust God and act in new ways. Most of our old trust had involved hedging our bets, just in case wealth and worldly power are really all they claim. Or we had worked out elaborate schemes of living in two worlds: one driven by worldly powers and the other by the so-called religious virtues.

But now those strategies must come to an end. There can be no two-timing, no lukewarm dabbling in religion, but only the embrace of the new reality Christ announces. Consider again the temptations of Jesus in Matthew and Luke: trusting monetary gain rather than God, trying to manipulate God for our ends, or giving our loyalty to the status quo (which means the oppressive powers of the world). Now these temptations are exposed for what they are: centering our lives in things of this world, which become the means of exclusion and violence. By rejecting them and embodying the new life, Jesus exposes the powers of this world for what they are, namely, forms of death. Their power has been broken. So he declares to James and John, who still want to hang on to worldly power: "It shall not be so among you." Or St. Paul declares, having described the new reality in Christ, that we live in a new time. So he admonishes the listeners with the words: "From now on, therefore . . ." This is the time in which we live, not a year, month, or day marked by the calendar, not an hour measured in relation to Greenwich, England, but a time marked by the announcement of the rule of God and the breaking of the world's hold over us. It is "From now on, therefore!"

2. In such a new time, repentance and trust mean that we confess that we have been co-conspirators and collaborators with the powers of this world. We were born into a world already at war and we willingly embraced the divisive and oppressive forces. As one prayer says, we must confess the evil done on our behalf. Thus there can no longer be any feigned innocence regarding our relations with other people or our reading of American history. Whether we are direct descendants of colonists, or claim relatives who arrived much later, we have been the benefactors of the sufferings of numerous peoples. And what we call business as usual continues the abuse of so many people. Stepping into the new reality, therefore, can only mean that we enter into something that is so new that St. John suggests it is like a new birth and St. Paul suggests it is like dying and rising. It is indeed a turning from our old life and a turning toward the Kingdom of God.

3. To turn toward God is to know that we have been claimed by God. The discovery of grace—whether first experienced in the acceptance by family, friendship, or the love of another person—is a liberating moment. Grace removes the need to prove oneself or live in the danger of losing oneself. In grace God declares that we are accepted; our value and worth are secure in God's declaration, even against our worst fears. When Luther continued to be tormented by the fear of his unworthiness, he was advised to stop the endless introspection or the attempts to prove himself, but instead look to the cross. There in the form of the crucified we see the grace of God.

If then our lives have been reformed as a gift of God, let us live without claims. Here I am drawing on St. Paul's judgment against the Corinthian church, engaged in endless divisions because of competing claims to wisdom and spiritual power. Since these are the very things that produce the crucifixion of the innocent the world over, Paul says such claiming must stop. We have no claims which may be the basis of our standing before God except that God has loved and claimed us in Christ. There can be no doubt that this is almost unimaginable. How could one live in this world without relying on our achievements, our moral rectitude, our social and political status? (Writing in an election year, this is indeed hard to imagine!) But Paul is serious. Whatever we have or whatever we do, these are gifts from God, not to be used to gain advantage over others but to be used in the service of God and neighbor. One thing is clear: there can be no freedom in Christ, no security in being claimed by God, until we are willing to give up the divisive and harmful claims of this world. This is the meaning of the peace of Christ: we who are so different and divided are brought together in spite of our former claims, to be united at the table of our Lord.

4. From the perspective of the peace of Christ we can now see the world as God's creation. I once spoke to a class about the Christian view of God and environmental ethics. When I finished a student did not get the connection and wondered why we bother with broad theological concepts. So I took the class to the chapel, where I asked them to sing a wonderful arrangement of Psalm 95. It begins with the resounding affirmation: "O Come let us sing to the Lord, let us make a joyful noise to the rock of our salvation . . ." Then in verse 5 it declares: "The sea is God's, for God made it . . ." When we concluded I said: "The sea is God's, it does not belong to the oil companies." To be claimed by grace is to see the whole world as the creation of God possessing intrinsic value. When we say that God created all people, it binds us together as brothers and sisters.

From this vantage point we must repent of our attachment to things and practices that do not make for life but only destruction. We already know what these are. While we seem quite willing to accept the gifts of the new creation for ourselves, we are unwilling to extend to others these same gifts that make for life. But in the community of Christ the wall between us and them is broken down. From repentance and trust comes a rebirth of justice and compassion: the grace extended to us is shared with all people.

To see the world as God's creation is to see all things in God. At various points in these discussions I have used the image of centering. In our old life, we have known how life can be centered in ourselves or in things of this world, to our detriment. In grace we discover that life can be centered in God. The surprising thing about such a recentering is that it is not the loss of our life but the affirmation of our life as it was meant to be. As argued earlier, this means a rejection of the dualism of the religious life separated from the secular life. It is the road not taken by Augustine, as he assumed that the only way to give himself to God was to forsake life in the world. By contrast I believe repentance and trust call us not to forsake the world but to embody new relations of love and justice in life together.

5. Finally, to have faith is to see the unfolding of God's glory. This means celebrating our life together in the peace of Christ. We are not meant to live alone but in community. One community can only be true to its calling by reaching out to other communities. It also means to ask what God is doing in the world. Only by asking this question can we discover a purpose for our lives that transcends the limits of one life or even the life of one group. The purpose and mission of the church is already announced in the new reality of Christ: to participate in the reconciliation of all people, to celebrate the freedom of Christ in the face of oppressive powers, to be servants of those in need and care for the sick and dying, and to rejoice in the worship of God. We can and should expect precisely what God has promised: the forgiveness of sins, freedom from the power of death, reconciliation in the name of Christ, hope, peace, and joy. These are the gifts of God present in the world.

Over the years I have often heard the comment: "I want to make a difference." Some have been critical of this, since it may sound very presumptuous. Which of us can possibly claim to do that in our life? But there is another way of looking at the statement. In a world where Americans are well known for being practical and concerned about this world rather than heavenly realms, the comment may well represent a secularized yearning for salvation. It may be an expression of hope for something good and new.

We want to identify with, and give our lives to, causes and movements that will embody justice and life. That such yearning has not always drawn people into churches is understandable, given the ways in which churches have failed people and do not appear to be the places where the real action is taking place. I think I have made clear that I understand the caution some might have in seeing the church as the difference-maker. But I still believe the community of Christ embodies Christ to the world. Even more important, I also believe Christ is first in the world. Christ is whenever two or three gather in his name, but also already there when people struggle for justice and peace, wherever the innocent suffer for

Conclusion

righteousness' sake. It is central to Christian faith that we can make a difference by participating in the unfolding glory of God in the world. God gathers together all our efforts. As they reflect the new life in Christ they become the light of the world.

www.ingramcontent.com/pod-product-compliance
Lightning Source LLC
Chambersburg PA
CBHW030904170426
43193CB00009BA/731